Everyday Cooking
made simple

Publications International, Ltd.

Photographs on front cover and page 21 © Shutterstock.com.

Pictured on the front cover: Everyday Chicken Salad *(page 20)*.

Pictured on the back cover *(clockwise from top left):* Cauliflower, Sausage and Gouda Sheet Pan *(page 87)*, Southwestern Flatbread with Black Beans and Corn *(page 129)* and Fettuccine alla Carbonara *(page 164)*.

ISBN: 978-1-63938-300-9

Manufactured in China.

8 7 6 5 4 3 2 1

Microwave Cooking: Microwave ovens vary in wattage. Use the cooking times as guidelines and check for doneness before adding more time.

Let's get social!
 @Publications_International
@PublicationsInternational
www.pilbooks.com

Contents

Salads

Caprese Quinoa Salad
makes 6 servings

1 cup uncooked quinoa

2 cups water

½ teaspoon salt

½ cup balsamic vinaigrette

1 container (about 10 ounces) grape tomatoes

⅓ cup chopped fresh basil

1 clove garlic, minced

⅛ teaspoon black pepper

1 package (8 ounces) fresh mozzarella pearls (small balls)

1 Place quinoa in fine-mesh strainer; rinse well under cold water.

2 Bring 2 cups water to a boil in medium saucepan over high heat; stir in quinoa and salt. Reduce heat to low; cover and simmer 10 to 15 minutes or until quinoa is tender and water is absorbed.

3 Remove from heat; fluff quinoa with fork. Let stand 5 minutes to cool slightly. Transfer to serving bowl.

4 Add vinaigrette, tomatoes, basil, garlic, pepper and cheese; toss gently to blend.

Greek Salad
makes 6 servings

Salad

- 3 medium tomatoes, cut into 8 wedges each
- 1 green bell pepper, cut into 1-inch pieces
- ½ English cucumber (8 to 10 inches), quartered lengthwise and sliced crosswise
- ½ red onion, thinly sliced
- ½ cup pitted Kalamata olives
- 1 block (8 ounces) feta cheese, cut into ½-inch cubes

Dressing

- 6 tablespoons extra virgin olive oil
- 3 tablespoons red wine vinegar
- 1 to 2 cloves garlic, minced
- ¾ teaspoon dried oregano
- ¾ teaspoon salt
- ¼ teaspoon black pepper

1 For salad, combine tomatoes, bell pepper, cucumber, onion and olives in large bowl. Top with cheese.

2 For dressing, whisk oil, vinegar, garlic, oregano, salt and black pepper in small bowl until well blended. Pour over salad; stir gently to coat.

Shrimp and Soba Noodle Salad
makes 4 servings

4 ounces soba noodles*

2 teaspoons vegetable oil

2 cups diagonally sliced green beans (bite-size pieces)

1½ cups sliced mushrooms

2 tablespoons orange juice

2 tablespoons lime juice

1 tablespoon reduced-sodium soy sauce

2 teaspoons dark sesame oil

1½ cups (6 ounces) cooked medium shrimp

¼ cup thinly sliced red bell pepper

2 tablespoons finely chopped fresh cilantro

1 to 2 tablespoons toasted sesame seeds (optional)

Soba is a Japanese noodle made from buckwheat flour which can be found in Asian markets or the Asian section of most supermarkets. If unavailable, substitute linguine; cook according to package directions.

1 Cook noodles according to package directions; drain and rinse under warm water. Drain again and transfer to large bowl.

2 Heat vegetable oil in large skillet over medium-high heat. Add green beans and mushrooms; cook 8 minutes or until mushrooms are lightly browned and beans are softened, stirring occasionally.

3 Meanwhile, whisk orange juice, lime juice, soy sauce and sesame oil in small bowl until well blended.

4 Combine noodles, shrimp, green bean mixture and bell pepper in large bowl. Pour dressing over salad; sprinkle with cilantro and sesame seeds, if desired. Toss gently to blend.

Strawberry Spinach Salad with Poppy Seed Dressing
makes 4 servings

- 2 tablespoons canola oil
- 2 tablespoons unseasoned rice vinegar or raspberry vinegar
- 2 teaspoons honey
- 1 teaspoon ground dry mustard
- ½ teaspoon poppy seeds
- ¼ teaspoon salt
- ⅛ teaspoon black pepper
- 6 cups baby spinach
- 8 strawberries, halved
- ¼ cup chopped pecans
- ¼ cup sliced red onion
- 2 ounces goat cheese, crumbled

1 Whisk oil, vinegar, honey, mustard, poppy seeds, salt and pepper in small bowl until well blended.

2 Divide spinach among four plates; top with strawberries, pecans, onion and cheese.

3 Drizzle dressing over salads.

Salads

Mediterranean Chicken and Pasta Salad
makes 4 servings

8 ounces uncooked multigrain rotini pasta

3 cups diced cooked chicken

1 cup chopped roasted red peppers

½ cup pitted Kalamata olives, halved

¼ cup extra virgin olive oil

2 tablespoons cider vinegar

2 cloves garlic, minced

1½ teaspoons dried basil

½ teaspoon salt

1 Cook pasta according to package directions. Drain well; cool to room temperature.

2 Combine chicken, roasted peppers, olives, oil, vinegar, garlic, basil and salt in large bowl; mix well.

3 Add cooled pasta to chicken mixture; toss gently to coat.

Salsa Salad Bowl
makes 4 servings

1 can (about 15 ounces) black beans, rinsed and drained

1 pint cherry or grape tomatoes, quartered

4 ounces mozzarella cheese, cut into ¼-inch cubes

½ medium poblano pepper or green bell pepper, chopped

½ cup chopped red onion

⅓ cup chopped fresh cilantro

¼ cup lime juice (juice of 2 medium limes)

1 tablespoon extra virgin olive oil

¼ teaspoon salt

⅛ teaspoon ground red pepper

1 Combine beans, tomatoes, cheese, poblano pepper, onion and cilantro in medium bowl; mix well.

2 Whisk lime juice, oil, salt and red pepper in small bowl until well blended.

3 Pour dressing over salad; toss gently to coat.

Orzo Salad With Zucchini and Feta
makes 4 to 6 servings

1 cup uncooked orzo

3 tablespoons extra virgin olive oil, divided

2 cups coarsely chopped zucchini

1 cup finely chopped fresh Italian parsley

⅔ cup crumbled feta cheese

½ cup thinly sliced radishes

¼ cup thinly sliced green onions

2 tablespoons lemon juice

½ teaspoon salt

¼ teaspoon black pepper

1 Cook orzo according to package directions; drain and rinse under cold water to stop cooking. Transfer to large bowl.

2 Meanwhile heat 1 tablespoon oil in large skillet over medium heat. Add zucchini; cook and stir about 3 minutes or until slightly softened.

3 Add zucchini to orzo with parsley, cheese, radishes and green onions; stir gently to blend.

4 Whisk remaining 2 tablespoons oil, lemon juice, salt and pepper in small bowl until well blended. Pour dressing over salad; toss gently to coat.

Shrimp and Bulgur Salad
makes 2 servings

¾ cup water

6 tablespoons uncooked bulgur wheat

2 medium plum tomatoes, diced

1 small red bell pepper, diced

6 ounces cooked salad shrimp

¼ cup crumbled feta cheese

¼ cup chopped green onions

⅛ teaspoon salt

⅛ teaspoon black pepper

1 tablespoon olive oil

1½ tablespoons white wine vinegar

2 tablespoons vegetable juice

1 Bring ¾ cup water to a boil in small saucepan over high heat. Stir in bulgur. Reduce heat to low; cover and cook 5 minutes. Remove from heat; let stand, covered, 10 minutes.

2 Combine tomatoes, bell pepper, shrimp, cheese, green onions, salt and pepper in medium bowl. Gently stir in bulgur.

3 Whisk oil, vinegar and vegetable juice in small bowl until well blended. Pour over salad; toss gently to coat.

Everyday Chicken Salad
makes 4 servings

Chicken

1½ teaspoons salt

1½ teaspoons dried basil

1 teaspoon garlic powder

1 teaspoon paprika

½ teaspoon black pepper

¼ to ½ teaspoon red
pepper flakes

3 tablespoons olive oil

4 boneless skinless
chicken breasts
(about 4 ounces each)

Salad

1 green onion, chopped

1 cup ranch or creamy
Italian salad dressing

8 cups mixed greens

½ cucumber, thinly sliced

1 ripe avocado, sliced

1 lemon, cut into wedges

1 Combine salt, basil, garlic powder, paprika, black pepper and red pepper flakes in large bowl; mix well. Reserve 1 teaspoon seasoning mixture; set aside.

2 Stir 1 tablespoon oil into remaining spice mixture. Add chicken; stir to coat.

3 Heat remaining 2 tablespoons oil in large skillet over medium-high heat. Add chicken; cook 5 to 6 minutes per side or until browned and no longer pink in center. Remove to cutting board; cool 5 minutes before slicing.

4 Stir green onions into dressing. Combine mixed greens, cucumber and avocado on serving plates; top with chicken. Sprinkle with reserved seasoning mixture; serve with dressing and lemon wedges.

Soups

One-Pot Chinese Chicken Soup

makes 4 servings

6 cups chicken broth

2 cups water

1 pound boneless skinless chicken thighs

⅓ cup reduced-sodium soy sauce

1 package (16 ounces) frozen stir-fry vegetables

6 ounces uncooked dried thin Chinese egg noodles

1 to 3 tablespoons sriracha sauce

1 Combine broth, water, chicken and soy sauce in medium saucepan; bring to a boil over high heat. Reduce heat to low; cover and simmer 20 minutes or until chicken is cooked through and very tender. Remove chicken to plate; let stand until cool enough to handle.

2 Meanwhile, add vegetables and noodles to broth in saucepan; bring to a boil over high heat. Reduce heat to medium-high; cook 5 minutes or until noodles are tender and vegetables are heated through, stirring occasionally.

3 Shred chicken into bite-size pieces. Stir chicken and 1 tablespoon sriracha into soup; taste and add additional sriracha for a spicier flavor.

West African Peanut Soup
makes 6 to 8 servings

2 tablespoons vegetable oil

1 large onion, chopped

½ cup chopped roasted peanuts

1½ tablespoons minced fresh ginger

4 cloves garlic, minced (about 1 tablespoon)

1 teaspoon salt

4 cups vegetable broth

2 sweet potatoes, peeled and cut into ½-inch pieces

1 can (28 ounces) whole tomatoes, drained and coarsely chopped

¼ teaspoon ground red pepper

1 bunch Swiss chard or kale, stemmed and shredded

⅓ cup unsweetened peanut butter (creamy or chunky)

1 Heat oil in large saucepan over medium-high heat. Add onion; cook and stir 5 minutes or until softened. Add peanuts, ginger, garlic and salt; cook and stir 1 minute.

2 Stir in broth, sweet potatoes, tomatoes and red pepper; bring to a boil. Reduce heat to medium; cook 10 minutes.

3 Stir in chard and peanut butter; simmer over medium-low heat 10 minutes or until vegetables are tender and soup is creamy.

Sausage Rice Soup
makes 4 to 6 servings

2 teaspoons olive oil

8 ounces Italian sausage, casings removed

1 small onion, chopped

½ teaspoon fennel seeds

1 tablespoon tomato paste

4 cups chicken broth

1 can (about 14 ounces) whole tomatoes, undrained, crushed with hands or coarsely chopped

1½ cups water

½ cup uncooked rice

¼ teaspoon salt

⅛ teaspoon black pepper

2 to 3 ounces baby spinach

⅓ cup shredded mozzarella cheese (optional)

1 Heat oil in large saucepan or Dutch oven over medium-high heat. Add sausage; cook 8 minutes or until browned, stirring to break up meat. Add onion; cook and stir 5 minutes or until softened. Add fennel seeds; cook and stir 30 seconds. Add tomato paste; cook and stir 1 minute.

2 Stir in broth, tomatoes with juice, water, rice, ¼ teaspoon salt and ⅛ teaspoon pepper; bring to a boil. Reduce heat to medium-low; simmer 18 minutes or until rice is tender. Stir in spinach; cook 3 minutes or until wilted. Season with additional salt and pepper.

3 Sprinkle with cheese, if desired, just before serving.

Pasta e Ceci
makes 4 servings

4 tablespoons olive oil, divided

1 onion, chopped

1 carrot, chopped

1 clove garlic, minced

1 sprig fresh rosemary

1 teaspoon salt, plus additional for seasoning

1 can (28 ounces) whole tomatoes, drained and crushed (see Tip)

2 cups vegetable broth

1 can (about 15 ounces) chickpeas, undrained

1 bay leaf

⅛ teaspoon red pepper flakes

1 cup uncooked orecchiette pasta

Black pepper (optional)

Chopped fresh parsley or basil (optional)

1 Heat 3 tablespoons oil in large saucepan over medium-high heat. Add onion and carrot; cook 10 minutes or until vegetables are soft, stirring occasionally.

2 Add garlic, rosemary and 1 teaspoon salt; cook and stir 1 minute. Stir in tomatoes, broth, chickpeas with liquid, bay leaf and red pepper flakes. Remove 1 cup mixture to food processor or blender; process until smooth. Stir back into saucepan; bring to a boil.

3 Stir in pasta. Reduce heat to medium; cook 12 to 15 minutes or until pasta is tender and mixture is creamy. Remove and discard bay leaf and rosemary sprig. Taste and season with additional salt and black pepper, if desired.

4 Divide evenly among bowls; drizzle with remaining 1 tablespoon oil and sprinkle with parsley, if desired.

Tip

To crush the tomatoes, take them out of the can one at a time and crush them between your fingers over the pot. Or coarsely chop them with a knife.

Spicy Thai Coconut Soup
makes 4 servings

2 **cups chicken broth**

1 **can (13½ ounces) light coconut milk**

1 **tablespoon minced fresh ginger**

½ **to 1 teaspoon red curry paste**

3 **cups coarsely shredded cooked chicken (about 12 ounces)**

1 **can (15 ounces) straw mushrooms, drained**

1 **can (about 8 ounces) baby corn, drained**

2 **tablespoons lime juice**

¼ **cup chopped fresh cilantro**

1 Combine broth, coconut milk, ginger and curry paste in large saucepan; mix well. Add chicken, mushrooms and corn; bring to a simmer over medium heat. Cook until heated through, stirring occasionally.

2 Stir in lime juice. Sprinkle with cilantro just before serving.

Note

Red curry paste can be found in jars in the Asian food section of large grocery stores. Spice levels can vary between brands—start with ½ teaspoon, then add more as desired.

Middle Eastern Lentil Soup

makes 4 servings

1 cup dried lentils

2 tablespoons olive oil

1 small onion, chopped

1 medium red bell pepper, chopped

1 teaspoon whole fennel seeds

½ teaspoon ground cumin

¼ teaspoon ground red pepper

4 cups water

½ teaspoon salt

1 tablespoon lemon juice

½ cup plain yogurt

2 tablespoons chopped fresh parsley

1 Rinse lentils, discarding any debris or blemished lentils. Drain.

2 Heat oil in large saucepan over medium-high heat. Add onion and bell pepper; cook and stir 5 minutes or until vegetables are tender. Add fennel seeds, cumin and red pepper; cook and stir 1 minute.

3 Add water, lentils and salt; bring to a boil. Reduce heat to low; cover and simmer 25 to 30 minutes or until lentils are tender. Stir in lemon juice.

4 Top each serving with yogurt; sprinkle with parsley.

Serving Suggestion:

Serve with homemade pita chips. Cut four pita bread rounds into six wedges each; toss with 1 tablespoon olive oil and 1 teaspoon coarse salt. Spread on large baking sheet; bake at 350°F 15 minutes or until lightly browned and crisp.

Quick and Easy Ravioli Soup
makes 6 to 8 servings

8 ounces mild Italian sausage, casings removed

½ cup chopped onion

1 clove garlic, crushed

2 cans (about 14 ounces each) chicken broth

2 cups water

1 package (9 ounces) frozen mini cheese-filled ravioli

1 can (about 15 ounces) chickpeas, rinsed and drained

1 can (about 14 ounces) diced tomatoes with mild green chiles

¾ teaspoon dried oregano

½ teaspoon black pepper

1 cup baby spinach

Grated Parmesan cheese

1 Cook sausage, onion and garlic 5 minutes in large saucepan or Dutch oven over medium heat, stirring to break up meat. Drain fat. Transfer to medium bowl.

2 Add broth and water to saucepan; bring to a boil over medium-high heat. Add ravioli; cook 4 to 5 minutes or until tender.

3 Stir in sausage mixture, chickpeas, tomatoes, oregano and pepper; cook 3 minutes or until heated through. Stir in spinach; cook 1 minute or until wilted. Sprinkle with cheese.

Hot and Sour Soup
makes 4 servings

2 cans (about 14 ounces each) chicken broth

1 can (4 ounces) sliced mushrooms

2 tablespoons rice vinegar or white wine vinegar

¼ to ½ teaspoon hot pepper sauce

2 tablespoons soy sauce

2 tablespoons cornstarch

1 egg, lightly beaten

2 green onions, thinly sliced, plus additional for garnish

Thinly sliced red chile pepper (optional)

1 Combine broth, mushrooms, vinegar and hot pepper sauce in medium saucepan; bring to a boil over high heat.

2 Stir soy sauce into cornstarch in small bowl until smooth. Add to saucepan; cook and stir over medium-high heat until soup is slightly thickened.

3 Gradually pour in egg, stirring constantly in one direction 1 minute or until egg is cooked. Remove from heat; stir in two green onions. Garnish with additional green onion and chile pepper.

Tip

For a heartier soup, add shredded cooked chicken to the broth before thickening it.

Pasta e Fagioli
makes 8 servings

2 tablespoons olive oil

1 cup chopped onion

3 cloves garlic, minced

2 cans (about 14 ounces each) Italian-style stewed tomatoes, undrained

3 cups vegetable broth

1 can (about 15 ounces) cannellini beans,* undrained

¼ cup chopped fresh Italian parsley

1 teaspoon dried basil

½ teaspoon salt

¼ teaspoon black pepper

4 ounces uncooked small shell pasta

If cannellini beans are unavailable, substitute Great Northern beans.

1 Heat oil in large saucepan or Dutch oven over medium heat. Add onion and garlic; cook and stir 5 minutes or until onion is tender.

2 Stir in tomatoes, broth, beans with liquid, parsley, basil, salt and pepper; bring to a boil over high heat. Reduce heat to low; cover and simmer 10 minutes.

3 Stir in pasta; cover and cook over medium heat 10 minutes or just until pasta is tender. Serve immediately.

Greek Lemon and Rice Soup
makes 4 to 6 servings

2 tablespoons butter

⅓ cup minced green onions

6 cups chicken broth

⅔ cup uncooked long grain rice

4 eggs

Juice of 1 lemon

⅛ teaspoon black pepper (optional)

Fresh mint and lemon peel (optional)

1 Melt butter in large saucepan over medium heat. Add green onions; cook and stir about 3 minutes or until tender.

2 Stir in broth and rice; bring to a boil over medium-high heat. Reduce heat to low; cover and simmer 20 to 25 minutes or until rice is tender.

3 Beat eggs in medium bowl. Stir in lemon juice and ½ cup hot broth mixture until blended. Gradually pour egg mixture into broth mixture in saucepan, stirring constantly. Cook and stir over low heat 2 to 3 minutes or until soup thickens enough to lightly coat spoon. *Do not boil.*

4 Stir in pepper, if desired. Garnish with mint and lemon peel.

Poultry

Barbecue Chicken Pizza
makes 4 servings

1 package (16 ounces) refrigerated pizza dough

1 tablespoon olive oil

6 ounces boneless skinless chicken breasts, cut into strips (about 2×¼ inch)

¼ teaspoon salt

⅛ teaspoon black pepper

6 tablespoons barbecue sauce, divided

⅔ cup shredded mozzarella cheese, divided

½ cup shredded smoked Gouda cheese, divided

½ small red onion, cut vertically into ⅛-inch slices

2 tablespoons chopped fresh cilantro

1 Preheat oven to 450°F. Line baking sheet with parchment paper. Let dough come to room temperature.

2 Heat oil in large skillet over medium-high heat. Season chicken with salt and pepper; cook 5 minutes or just until cooked though, stirring occasionally. Remove chicken to medium bowl. Add 2 tablespoons barbecue sauce; stir to coat.

3 Roll out dough into 12-inch circle on lightly floured surface. Transfer to prepared baking sheet. Spread remaining 4 tablespoons barbecue sauce over dough, leaving ½-inch border. Sprinkle with 2 tablespoons mozzarella and 2 tablespoons Gouda. Top with chicken and onion; sprinkle with remaining cheeses.

4 Bake 12 to 15 minutes or until crust is browned and cheese is bubbly. Sprinkle with cilantro.

Zesty Italian Chicken Bites >
makes 4 servings

2 **boneless skinless chicken breasts (about 6 ounces each)**

¼ **cup zesty Italian salad dressing**

2 **garlic cloves, minced**

½ **teaspoon salt**

¼ **teaspoon black pepper**

1 Cut chicken into 1-inch pieces; place in large resealable food storage bag.

2 Combine dressing, garlic, salt and pepper in medium bowl; mix well. Pour over chicken; seal bag and turn to coat. Marinate in refrigerator 30 minutes to 1 hour.

3 Heat large skillet over medium-high heat; spray with nonstick cooking spray. Remove chicken from marinade; discard marinade. Add chicken to skillet; cook 5 minutes per side or until cooked through.

Mini Turkey Loaves
makes 4 servings

1 **pound ground turkey**

1 **small apple, chopped**

½ **small onion, chopped**

½ **cup old-fashioned oats**

2 **teaspoons Dijon mustard**

1 **teaspoon dried rosemary**

1 **teaspoon salt**

⅛ **teaspoon black pepper**

½ **to ¾ cup cranberry sauce**

1 Preheat oven to 425°F. Spray 12 standard (2½-inch) muffin cups with nonstick cooking spray.

2 Combine turkey, apple, onion, oats, mustard, rosemary, salt and pepper in large bowl; mix just until combined. Press evenly into prepared muffin cups.

3 Bake 20 minutes or until lightly browned and cooked through (165°F). Top with cranberry sauce.

Chicken Adobo
makes 6 servings

½ **cup cider vinegar**

½ **cup reduced-sodium soy sauce**

4 **cloves garlic, minced**

3 **bay leaves**

1 **teaspoon black pepper**

2½ **pounds bone-in skin-on chicken thighs (about 6)**

Hot cooked rice (optional)

Sliced green onion (optional)

1 Combine vinegar, soy sauce, garlic, bay leaves and pepper in large saucepan or deep skillet; mix well. Add chicken; turn to coat. Arrange chicken skin side down in liquid.

2 Bring to a boil over high heat. Reduce heat to low; cover and simmer 30 minutes. Turn chicken skin side up; simmer, uncovered, 20 minutes.

3 Preheat broiler. Line baking sheet with foil.

4 Remove chicken to prepared baking sheet, skin side up. Broil 6 minutes or until skin is browned and crisp. Meanwhile, cook liquid in saucepan over high heat 10 minutes or until reduced and slightly thickened.

5 Serve sauce over chicken and rice, if desired. Garnish with green onion.

Poultry

Simple Roasted Chicken
makes 4 servings

1 whole chicken
(about 4 pounds)

3 tablespoons butter,
softened

1½ teaspoons salt

1 teaspoon onion powder

1 teaspoon dried thyme

½ teaspoon garlic powder

½ teaspoon paprika

½ teaspoon black pepper

Fresh parsley sprigs
and lemon wedges
(optional)

1 Preheat oven to 425°F. Pat chicken dry; place in medium baking dish or on baking sheet.

2 Combine butter, salt, onion powder, thyme, garlic powder, paprika and pepper in small microwavable bowl; mash with fork until well blended. Loosen skin on chicken breasts and thighs; spread about one third of butter mixture under skin.

3 Microwave remaining butter mixture until melted. Brush melted butter mixture all over outside of chicken and inside cavity. Tie drumsticks together with kitchen string and tuck wing tips under.

4 Roast 20 minutes. *Reduce oven temperature to 375°F.* Roast 45 to 55 minutes or until chicken is cooked through (165°F), basting once with pan juices during last 10 minutes of cooking time. Remove chicken to large cutting board; tent with foil. Let stand 15 minutes before carving. Garnish with parsley and lemon wedges.

Southwestern Chicken and Black Bean Skillet
makes 4 servings

1 teaspoon ground cumin

1 teaspoon chili powder

½ teaspoon salt

4 boneless skinless chicken breasts (about 6 ounces each)

1 tablespoon canola or vegetable oil

1 onion, chopped

1 red bell pepper, chopped

1 can (about 15 ounces) black beans, rinsed and drained

½ cup chunky salsa

Lime wedges

¼ cup chopped fresh cilantro or green onions (optional)

1 Combine cumin, chili powder and salt in small bowl; sprinkle over both sides of chicken.

2 Heat oil in large skillet over medium-high heat. Add chicken; cook about 3 minutes per side or until browned. Remove to plate.

3 Add onion to skillet; cook and stir 1 minute. Add bell pepper; cook 5 minutes, stirring occasionally. Stir in beans and salsa.

4 Place chicken on top of bean mixture; cover and cook 6 to 7 minutes or until chicken is no longer pink in center. Serve with lime wedges; garnish with cilantro.

Chicken Fajita Roll-Ups
makes 4 servings

1 cup ranch dressing

1 teaspoon chili powder

2 tablespoons vegetable oil, divided

2 teaspoons lime juice

2 teaspoons fajita seasoning mix

½ teaspoon chipotle chili powder

¼ teaspoon salt

4 boneless skinless chicken breasts (about 6 ounces each)

4 fajita-size flour tortillas (8 to 9 inches)

1 cup (4 ounces) shredded Cheddar cheese

1 cup (4 ounces) shredded Monterey Jack cheese

3 cups shredded lettuce

1 cup pico de gallo

1 Combine ranch dressing and chili powder in small bowl; mix well. Refrigerate until ready to serve.

2 Whisk 1 tablespoon oil, lime juice, fajita seasoning mix, chipotle chili powder and salt until well blended. Coat both sides of chicken with spice mixture.

3 Heat remaining 1 tablespoon oil in large nonstick skillet or grill pan over medium-high heat. Add chicken; cook 6 minutes per side or until no longer pink in center. Remove to plate; let stand 5 minutes before slicing. Cut chicken breasts in half lengthwise, then cut crosswise into ½-inch strips.

4 Wipe out skillet with paper towel. Place one tortilla in skillet; sprinkle with ¼ cup Cheddar and ¼ cup Monterey Jack. Heat over medium heat until cheeses are melted. Remove tortilla to clean work surface or cutting board.

5 Sprinkle ¾ cup shredded lettuce down center of tortilla; top with ¼ cup pico de gallo and one fourth of chicken. Fold bottom of tortilla up over filling, then fold in sides and roll up. Cut in half diagonally. Repeat with remaining tortillas, cheese and fillings. Serve with ranch dipping sauce.

Turkey Vegetable Chili Mac
makes 4 servings

1 tablespoon vegetable oil

12 ounces ground turkey

½ cup chopped onion

2 cloves garlic, minced

1 can (about 15 ounces)
   black beans, rinsed
   and drained

1 can (about 14 ounces)
   Mexican-style stewed
   tomatoes, undrained

1 can (about 14 ounces)
   diced tomatoes

1 cup frozen corn

1 teaspoon Mexican
   seasoning

½ teaspoon salt

½ cup uncooked
   elbow macaroni

⅓ cup sour cream

   Finely chopped fresh
   cilantro or green
   onions (optional)

1 Heat oil in large saucepan or Dutch oven over medium heat. Add turkey, onion and garlic; cook and stir 5 minutes or until turkey is no longer pink.

2 Stir in beans, tomatoes with juice, diced tomatoes, corn, Mexican seasoning and salt; bring to a boil over high heat. Reduce heat to low; cover and simmer 15 minutes, stirring occasionally.

3 Meanwhile, cook pasta according to package directions. Drain pasta; stir into chili. Cook, uncovered, 2 to 3 minutes or until heated through.

4 Top with sour cream and cilantro, if desired.

Sheet Pan Chicken and Sausage Supper
makes about 6 servings

⅓ cup olive oil

2 tablespoons balsamic vinegar

1 teaspoon salt

1 teaspoon garlic powder

½ teaspoon black pepper

¼ teaspoon red pepper flakes

3 pounds bone-in chicken thighs and drumsticks

1 pound uncooked sweet Italian sausage (4 to 5 links), cut diagonally into 2-inch pieces

6 to 8 small red onions (about 1½ pounds), each cut into 6 wedges

3½ cups broccoli florets

1 Preheat oven to 425°F. Line baking sheet with foil, if desired.

2 Whisk oil, vinegar, salt, garlic powder, black pepper and red pepper flakes in small bowl until well blended. Combine chicken, sausage and onions on prepared baking sheet.

3 Drizzle with oil mixture; toss until well coated. Spread meat and onions in single layer (chicken thighs should be skin side up).

4 Bake 30 minutes. Add broccoli to baking sheet; stir to coat broccoli with pan juices and turn sausage. Bake 30 minutes or until broccoli is beginning to brown and chicken is cooked through (165°F).

Sesame Chicken
makes 4 servings

1 pound boneless skinless chicken breasts or thighs, cut into 1-inch pieces

⅔ cup teriyaki sauce, divided

2 teaspoons cornstarch

1 tablespoon peanut or vegetable oil

2 cloves garlic, minced

2 green onions, cut into ½-inch slices

1 tablespoon sesame seeds, toasted*

1 teaspoon dark sesame oil

To toast sesame seeds, cook in small skillet over medium-low heat 3 minutes or until seeds begin to pop and turn golden, stirring frequently.

1 Combine chicken and ⅓ cup teriyaki sauce in medium bowl; toss to coat. Marinate in refrigerator 15 to 20 minutes.

2 Drain chicken; discard marinade. Stir remaining ⅓ cup teriyaki sauce into cornstarch in small bowl until smooth.

3 Heat peanut oil in large skillet or wok over medium-high heat. Add chicken and garlic; cook and stir 3 minutes or until chicken is cooked through.

4 Stir cornstarch mixture; add to skillet. Cook and stir 1 minute or until sauce boils and thickens. Stir in green onions, sesame seeds and sesame oil.

Chicken Mirabella
makes 4 servings

4 boneless skinless
  chicken breasts
  (about 6 ounces each)

½ cup pitted prunes

½ cup assorted pitted
  olives (black, green
  or a combination)

¼ cup dry white wine or
  white grape juice

2 tablespoons olive oil

1 tablespoon capers

1 tablespoon red wine
  vinegar

1 teaspoon salt

1 teaspoon dried oregano

1 clove garlic, minced

1 tablespoon chopped
  fresh parsley, plus
  additional for garnish

2 teaspoons packed
  brown sugar

1 Preheat oven to 350°F.

2 Place chicken in 8-inch baking dish. Combine
  prunes, olives, wine, oil, capers, vinegar, salt,
  oregano, garlic and 1 tablespoon parsley in
  medium bowl; mix well. Pour over chicken;
  sprinkle with brown sugar.

3 Bake 25 to 30 minutes or until chicken is
  no longer pink in center, basting with sauce
  halfway through cooking. Garnish with
  additional parsley.

Tip

For more intense flavor, marinate the chicken
in the refrigerator at least 8 hours or overnight.
Sprinkle with brown sugar just before baking.

Chicken and Bean Tostadas
makes 4 servings

1 tablespoon vegetable oil

12 ounces boneless skinless chicken breasts, cut into ¾-inch pieces

1 green, red or yellow bell pepper, diced

1 cup chopped onion

2 teaspoons ground cumin

1 cup chunky salsa, divided

½ teaspoon salt

1 can (about 15 ounces) refried beans

8 tostada shells

¼ cup chopped fresh cilantro or green onion

1 Heat oil in large skillet over medium heat. Add chicken, bell pepper, onion and cumin; cook about 6 minutes or until chicken is no longer pink, stirring occasionally.

2 Stir in ¾ cup salsa and salt. Reduce heat to low; cook 5 to 6 minutes or until chicken is cooked through.

3 Meanwhile, combine refried beans and remaining ¼ cup salsa in microwavable bowl. Microwave on HIGH 3 minutes or until heated through, stirring occasionally.

4 Spread bean mixture over tostada shells; top with chicken mixture and cilantro.

Beef

Mongolian Beef
makes 4 servings

1¼ pounds beef flank steak

¼ cup cornstarch

3 tablespoons vegetable oil, divided

3 cloves garlic, minced

2 teaspoons grated fresh ginger

½ cup water

½ cup soy sauce

⅓ cup packed dark brown sugar

Pinch red pepper flakes

2 green onions, diagonally sliced into 1-inch pieces

Sesame seeds (optional)

Hot cooked rice (optional)

1 Cut flank steak in half lengthwise, then cut crosswise (against the grain) into ¼-inch slices. Combine beef and cornstarch in medium bowl; toss to coat.

2 Heat 1 tablespoon oil in large skillet or wok over high heat. Add half of beef in single layer (do not crowd); cook 1 to 2 minutes per side or until browned. Remove to clean bowl. Repeat with remaining beef and 1 tablespoon oil.

3 Heat remaining 1 tablespoon oil in same skillet over medium heat. Add garlic and ginger; cook and stir 30 seconds. Add water, soy sauce, brown sugar and red pepper flakes; bring to a boil, stirring until well blended. Cook 8 minutes or until sauce is slightly thickened, stirring occasionally.

4 Return beef to skillet; cook 2 to 3 minutes or until sauce thickens and beef is heated through. Stir in green onions. Sprinkle with sesame seeds; serve with rice, if desired.

Bacon and Blue Cheese Stuffed Burgers
makes 4 servings

4 slices bacon

1 small red onion,
   finely chopped

2 tablespoons crumbled
   blue cheese

1 tablespoon butter,
   softened

1½ pounds ground beef

   Salt and black pepper

4 onion or plain
   hamburger rolls

   Lettuce leaves

1 Cook bacon in large skillet over medium-high heat until almost crisp. Drain on paper towel-lined plate. Finely chop bacon; place in small bowl. Add onion to same skillet; cook and stir 5 minutes or until soft. Add to bowl with bacon; cool slightly. Stir in blue cheese and butter until well blended.

2 Prepare grill for direct cooking over medium-high heat. Spray grid with nonstick cooking spray.

3 Divide beef into eight portions. Flatten into thin patties about 4 inches wide; season with salt and pepper. Place 2 tablespoons bacon mixture in center of each of four patties; cover with remaining patties and pinch edges together to seal.

4 Grill patties, covered, over medium-high heat 4 to 5 minutes per side for medium doneness (160°F). Remove burgers to plate; let stand 2 minutes before serving. Serve burgers on rolls with lettuce.

Tip

For juicy, flavorful burgers, don't flatten the patties during cooking. Pressing down on the patties with a spatula not only squeezes out tasty juices, but with stuffed burgers, it might also cause the stuffing to pop out.

Taco-Topped Potatoes
makes 4 servings

4 Yukon Gold or red potatoes (about 6 ounces each), scrubbed and pierced with fork

8 ounces ground beef

½ (1¼-ounce) package taco seasoning mix

½ cup water

1 cup diced tomatoes

¼ teaspoon salt

2 cups shredded lettuce

½ cup (2 ounces) shredded sharp Cheddar cheese

¼ cup finely chopped green onions

½ cup sour cream

1 Microwave potatoes on HIGH 6 to 7 minutes or until fork-tender.

2 Cook beef in large skillet over medium-high heat 6 to 8 minutes or until browned, stirring to break up meat. Drain fat. Stir in seasoning mix and water; cook 3 minutes. Remove from heat.

3 Combine tomatoes and salt in medium bowl; mix well.

4 Split potatoes open and fluff with fork. Fill with beef mixture, tomatoes, lettuce, cheese and green onions. Serve with sour cream.

Balsamic Beef, Mushrooms and Onions
makes 4 servings

2 tablespoons olive oil, divided

2 large sweet onions, sliced

½ teaspoon salt, divided

5 teaspoons balsamic vinegar, divided

4 ounces (about 1 cup) mushrooms, sliced

1 boneless beef top sirloin (about 1 pound), cut into ½-inch slices

¼ teaspoon dried thyme

¼ teaspoon black pepper

1 Heat 1 tablespoon oil in large skillet over medium heat. Add onions; cook 15 minutes, stirring occsionally.

2 Stir in ¼ teaspoon salt. Add 3 teaspoons vinegar, 1 teaspoon at a time, scraping up browned bits from bottom of skillet.

3 Add mushrooms; cook over medium-low heat about 5 minutes or until tender, stirring occasionally. Transfer to medium bowl; cover to keep warm.

4 Add remaining 1 tablespoon oil to skillet; heat over medium-high heat. Add beef; sprinkle with remaining ¼ teaspoon salt, thyme and pepper. Cook 4 to 6 minutes or until browned, stirring occasionally.

5 Remove from heat; drizzle with remaining 2 teaspoons vinegar. Stir in vegetable mixture. Serve immediately.

Tamale Skillet Casserole
makes 4 servings

1 pound ground beef

1 cup frozen corn, thawed

1 can (4 ounces) diced green chiles

1 can (8 ounces) tomato sauce

½ cup water

1 package (about 1 ounce) taco seasoning mix

½ teaspoon ground cumin

½ cup biscuit baking mix

1 cup whole milk

2 eggs

1½ cups (6 ounces) shredded Monterey Jack cheese or Mexican cheese blend

Optional toppings: sour cream, sliced olives, chopped fresh tomatoes and chopped fresh cilantro

1 Preheat oven to 400°F. Cook beef in large ovenproof skillet over medium-high heat 6 to 8 minutes or until browned, stirring to break up meat. Drain fat.

2 Stir in corn, chiles, tomato sauce, water, taco seasoning mix and cumin; mix well. Remove from heat; smooth top of mixture into even layer with spoon.

3 Combine baking mix, milk and eggs in medium bowl; stir until well blended. Pour evenly over meat mixture.

4 Bake 40 minutes or until crust is golden brown and knife inserted into center comes out clean.

5 Sprinkle with cheese; let stand 5 minutes before serving. Serve with desired toppings.

Tri-Tip Roast with Spicy Potatoes
makes 6 servings

4 teaspoons chili powder

2 teaspoons dried oregano

½ teaspoon salt

3 pounds unpeeled
   red potatoes
   (about 9 potatoes)

3 tablespoons lime juice,
   divided

1 tablespoon olive oil

1 boneless lean beef loin
   tri-tip roast (about
   1¾ pounds)

1 Preheat oven to 425°F. Spray 13×9-inch baking dish with nonstick cooking spray. Combine chili powder, oregano and salt in small bowl; mix well.

2 Cut potatoes into wedges; place in large bowl. Add 2 tablespoons lime juice, oil and 1 tablespoon spice mixture; toss to coat. Spread potatoes in single layer in prepared baking dish.

3 Brush beef with remaining 1 tablespoon lime juice; rub with remaining spice mixture. Place beef on rack in roasting pan.

4 Place beef in center of oven; place potatoes beside or below beef. Roast 40 to 45 minutes or until center of beef reaches 140°F for medium or to desired doneness. Remove beef and potatoes from oven; tent with foil to keep warm. Let beef stand 10 minutes before slicing.

5 Thinly slice beef across the grain. Serve with potatoes.

Broccoli and Beef Pasta
makes 4 servings

1 pound ground beef

2 cloves garlic, minced

1 can (about 14 ounces) beef broth

1 onion, thinly sliced

1 cup uncooked rotini pasta

½ teaspoon dried basil

½ teaspoon dried oregano

½ teaspoon dried thyme

1 can (about 14 ounces) Italian-style diced tomatoes

2 cups broccoli florets *or* 1 package (10 ounces) frozen broccoli, thawed

¾ cup grated Parmesan cheese

1 Cook beef and garlic in large saucepan over medium-high heat 6 to 8 minutes or until browned, stirring to break up meat. Drain fat. Transfer to large bowl.

2 Add broth, onion, pasta, basil, oregano and thyme to saucepan; bring to a boil over high heat. Cook 6 minutes, stirring occasionally. Stir in tomatoes and broccoli; cook over medium-high heat 6 minutes or until broccoli is crisp-tender and pasta is tender, stirring occasionally.

3 Return beef to saucepan; cook 3 to 4 minutes or until heated through.

4 Transfer pasta, beef and vegetables to bowl with slotted spoon, leaving liquid in saucepan. Cover to keep warm.

5 Bring liquid left in saucepan to a boil over high heat; boil until thickened and reduced to 3 to 4 tablespoons. Spoon over pasta and vegetables; add cheese and stir gently to blend.

Greek-Style Steak Sandwiches
makes 4 servings

2 teaspoons Greek seasoning or dried oregano

1 beef flank steak (about 1½ pounds)

4 pita bread rounds, cut in half crosswise

1 small cucumber, thinly sliced

1 tomato, cut into thin wedges

½ cup sliced red onion

½ cup crumbled feta cheese

¼ cup red wine vinaigrette

1 cup plain yogurt

1 Rub Greek seasoning over both sides of steak. Place on plate; cover and refrigerate 30 to 60 minutes.

2 Prepare grill for direct cooking over medium heat.

3 Grill steak, covered, 8 to 10 minutes per side or to desired doneness. Remove steak to cutting board. Tent with foil; let stand 10 minutes before slicing.

4 Grill pita halves 1 minute per side or until warm.

5 Slice steak into thin strips against the grain. Divide meat among pita halves; top with cucumber, tomato, onion and cheese. Drizzle with vinaigrette; serve with yogurt.

Southwestern Sloppy Joes
makes 8 servings

1 pound ground beef

1 cup chopped onion

¼ cup chopped celery

¼ cup water

1 can (10 ounces) diced tomatoes and green chilies

1 can (8 ounces) tomato sauce

4 teaspoons packed brown sugar

½ teaspoon salt

½ teaspoon ground cumin

8 whole wheat hamburger buns, split

1 Cook beef, onion, celery and water in large skillet over medium heat 6 to 8 minutes or until beef is browned, stirring to break up meat.

2 Stir in tomatoes, tomato sauce, brown sugar, salt and cumin; bring to a boil over high heat. Reduce heat to low; simmer 20 minutes or until mixture is thickened. Serve on buns.

Spicy Chinese Pepper Steak
makes 4 servings

1 boneless beef top sirloin steak (about 1 pound), cut into thin strips

1 tablespoon cornstarch

3 cloves garlic, minced

½ teaspoon red pepper flakes

2 tablespoons peanut or canola oil, divided

1 green bell pepper, cut into thin strips

1 red bell pepper, cut into thin strips

¼ cup oyster sauce

2 tablespoons soy sauce

3 tablespoons chopped fresh cilantro or green onions

1 Combine beef, cornstarch, garlic and red pepper flakes in medium bowl; toss to coat.

2 Heat 1 tablespoon oil in large skillet or wok over medium-high heat. Add bell peppers; cook and stir 3 minutes. Remove to small bowl.

3 Add remaining 1 tablespoon oil and beef mixture to skillet; cook and stir 4 to 5 minutes or until beef is barely pink in center.

4 Add oyster sauce and soy sauce to skillet; cook and stir 1 minute. Return bell peppers to skillet; cook and stir 1 to 2 minutes or until sauce thickens. Sprinkle with cilantro.

Picadillo Tacos
makes 2 servings

6 ounces ground beef

½ cup chopped green bell pepper

½ teaspoon ground cumin

½ teaspoon chili powder

¼ teaspoon salt

⅛ teaspoon ground cinnamon

½ cup chunky salsa

1 tablespoon golden raisins

4 (6-inch) corn tortillas, warmed

½ cup shredded lettuce

¼ cup (1 ounce) shredded Cheddar cheese

1 small tomato, chopped

1 Combine beef, bell pepper, cumin, chili powder, salt and cinnamon in large skillet; cook over medium heat 5 minutes, stirring to break up meat. Drain fat.

2 Stir in salsa and raisins. Reduce heat to low; cook 5 minutes or until meat is cooked through, stirring occasionally.

3 Divide meat mixture evenly among tortillas; top with lettuce, cheese and tomato.

Pork

Cauliflower, Sausage and Gouda Sheet Pan
makes 6 servings

1 package (16 ounces) mushrooms, trimmed and halved

3 tablespoons olive oil, divided

1 teaspoon salt, divided

1 head cauliflower, separated into florets and thinly sliced

¼ teaspoon chipotle chili powder

1 package (about 13 ounces) smoked sausage, cut into ¼-inch slices

2 tablespoons peach or apricot preserves

1 tablespoon Dijon mustard

½ red onion, thinly sliced

6 ounces Gouda cheese, cubed

1 Preheat oven to 400°F.

2 Place mushrooms in medium bowl. Drizzle with 1 tablespoon oil and sprinkle with ½ teaspoon salt; toss to coat. Spread on baking sheet.

3 Combine cauliflower, remaining 2 tablespoons oil, ½ teaspoon salt and chipotle chili powder in same bowl; toss to coat. Spread on baking sheet with mushrooms.

4 Combine sausage, preserves and mustard in same bowl; stir until well coated. Arrange sausage over vegetables; top with onion.

5 Bake 30 minutes. Remove from oven; sprinkle cheese cubes over cauliflower. Bake 5 minutes or until cheese is melted and cauliflower is tender.

Pork Tenderloin with Cabbage and Leeks
makes 4 servings

¼ cup olive oil, plus additional for pan

1 teaspoon salt

¾ teaspoon garlic powder

½ teaspoon dried thyme

½ teaspoon black pepper

1 pork tenderloin (about 1¼ pounds)

½ medium savoy cabbage, cored and cut into ¼-inch slices (about 6 cups)

1 small leek, cut in half lengthwise then cut crosswise into ¼-inch diagonal slices

1 to 2 teaspoons cider vinegar

1. Preheat oven to 450°F. Brush baking sheet with oil.

2 Combine salt, garlic powder, thyme and pepper in small bowl; mix well. Whisk in ¼ cup oil until well blended. Brush pork with about 1 tablespoon oil mixture, turning to coat all sides.

3 Combine cabbage and leek in large bowl. Drizzle with remaining oil mixture; toss to coat. Spread on prepared baking sheet; top with pork.

4 Bake 25 minutes or until pork is 145°F, stirring cabbage mixture halfway through cooking time. Remove pork to cutting board; tent with foil. Let stand 10 minutes before slicing. Add vinegar to cabbage mixture; stir to blend.

Tip

If you can't find savoy cabbage, you can substitute regular green cabbage but it may take slightly longer to cook. If the cabbage is not crisp-tender when the pork is done, return the vegetables to the oven for 10 minutes or until crisp-tender.

Zesty Skillet Pork Chops
makes 4 servings

1 teaspoon chili powder

½ teaspoon salt, divided

4 boneless pork chops
  (about 6 ounces each)

2 cups diced tomatoes

1 cup chopped green, red
  or yellow bell pepper

¾ cup thinly sliced celery

½ cup chopped onion

1 teaspoon dried thyme

1 tablespoon hot pepper
  sauce

1 tablespoon vegetable oil

2 tablespoons finely
  chopped fresh parsley

1 Combine chili powder and ¼ teaspoon salt in small bowl; rub onto one side of pork chops.

2 Combine tomatoes, bell pepper, celery, onion, thyme and hot pepper sauce in medium bowl; mix well.

3 Heat oil in large skillet over medium-high heat. Add pork, seasoned side down; cook 1 minute. Turn pork and top with tomato mixture; bring to a boil. Reduce heat to low; cover and cook 25 minutes or until pork is tender and tomato mixture has thickened.

4 Remove pork to serving plates. Bring tomato mixture to a boil over high heat; cook 2 minutes or until most of liquid has evaporated. Remove from heat; stir in parsley and remaining ¼ teaspoon salt. Serve sauce over pork.

Spinach and Sausage Pizza
makes 4 servings

2 teaspoons olive oil

3 ounces (1 link) smoked sausage, thinly sliced

2 prepared whole wheat pizza crusts (about 5 ounces each)

½ cup ricotta cheese

1 clove garlic, crushed

½ teaspoon Italian seasoning

2 tablespoons grated Parmesan cheese

2 cups baby spinach, coarsely chopped

2 plum tomatoes, thinly sliced

¾ cup (3 ounces) shredded mozzarella cheese

1 Heat oil in large skillet over medium heat. Add sausage; cook until browned, stirring occasionally.

2 Preheat oven to 450°F. Place pizza crusts on baking sheet.

3 Combine ricotta, garlic, Italian seasoning and Parmesan in small bowl; mix well. Spread in thin layer over pizza crusts to within ½ inch of edge. Top with sausage, spinach, tomatoes and mozzarella.

4 Bake 12 to 15 minutes or until cheese is melted and golden brown and edges are crisp.

Easy Moo Shu Pork >

makes 2 servings

2 teaspoons vegetable oil

8 ounces pork tenderloin, cut into ½-inch strips

4 green onions, cut into ½-inch pieces

1½ cups packaged coleslaw mix

2 tablespoons hoisin sauce or Asian plum sauce

4 (8-inch) flour tortillas, warmed

1 Heat oil in large skillet medium-high heat. Add pork and green onions; cook and stir 2 to 3 minutes or until pork is barely pink in center. Stir in coleslaw mix and hoisin sauce.

2 Spoon pork mixture onto tortillas. Roll up tortillas, folding in sides to enclose filling.

Note

To warm tortillas, stack and wrap loosely in plastic wrap. Microwave on HIGH 15 to 20 seconds or until warm and pliable.

Quick Pork and Red Bean Chili

makes 4 servings

1 tablespoon canola or vegetable oil

1 pound pork tenderloin, cut into ½-inch pieces

4 cloves garlic, minced

2 teaspoons chili powder

1 can (about 15 ounces) red kidney beans, rinsed and drained

1 can (about 14 ounces) fire-roasted diced tomatoes

¾ cup spicy salsa

½ teaspoon salt

½ cup chopped fresh cilantro

1 Heat oil in large saucepan over medium heat. Add pork, garlic and chili powder; cook 4 minutes or until pork is browned on all sides, stirring occasionally.

2 Stir in beans, tomatoes, salsa and salt; bring to a boil over medium heat. Reduce heat to low; simmer, uncovered, 12 minutes or until pork is no longer pink in center. Top with cilantro.

Sausage and Peppers
makes 4 servings

1 pound uncooked hot or mild Italian sausage links

2 tablespoons olive oil

3 medium onions, cut into ½-inch slices

2 red bell peppers, cut into ½-inch slices

2 green bell peppers, cut into ½-inch slices

1½ teaspoons coarse salt, divided

1 teaspoon dried oregano

Italian rolls (optional)

1. Fill medium saucepan half full with water or beer; bring to a boil over high heat. Add sausage; cook 5 minutes over medium heat. Drain and cut diagonally into 1-inch slices.

2. Heat oil in large skillet over medium-high heat. Add sausage; cook about 10 minutes or until browned, stirring occasionally. Remove to plate.

3. Add onions, bell peppers, 1 teaspoon salt and oregano to skillet; cook over medium heat about 25 minutes or until vegetables are very soft and browned in spots, stirring occasionally.

4. Stir sausage and remaining ½ teaspoon salt into skillet; cook 3 minutes or until heated through. Serve with Italian rolls, if desired.

One-Pan Pork Fu Yung
makes 4 servings

1 cup chicken broth

1 tablespoon cornstarch

½ teaspoon dark sesame oil, divided

1 tablespoon vegetable oil

8 ounces pork tenderloin, chopped

1 cup sliced mushrooms

4 tablespoons thinly sliced green onions, divided

½ teaspoon salt

¼ teaspoon white pepper

1 cup bean sprouts

2 eggs

2 egg whites

1 Combine broth, cornstarch and ¼ teaspoon sesame oil in small saucepan; cook and stir over medium heat 5 to 6 minutes or until thickened. Keep sauce warm over low heat.

2 Heat vegetable oil in large nonstick skillet over medium-high heat. Add pork; cook and stir 4 minutes or until no longer pink. Add mushrooms, 2 tablespoons green onions, remaining ¼ teaspoon sesame oil, salt and pepper; cook and stir 4 to 5 minutes or until mushrooms are lightly browned. Add bean sprouts; cook and stir 1 minute. Gently flatten mixture in skillet with spatula.

3 Beat eggs and egg whites in medium bowl; pour over pork mixture. Reduce heat to low; cover and cook 3 minutes or until eggs are set.

4 Cut pork fu yung into four wedges. Top each wedge with ¼ cup sauce; sprinkle with remaining green onions.

Apple-Cherry Glazed Pork Chops
makes 2 servings

¼ teaspoon salt

¼ teaspoon dried thyme

⅛ teaspoon black pepper

2 boneless pork loin chops (about 4 ounces each)

2 teaspoons vegetable oil

⅔ cup unsweetened apple juice

½ small apple, sliced

2 tablespoons sliced green onion

2 tablespoons dried tart cherries

1 teaspoon cornstarch

1 tablespoon water

1 Combine salt, thyme and pepper in small bowl; mix well. Rub onto both sides of pork chops.

2 Heat oil in large skillet over medium heat. Add pork; cook 2 to 3 minutes per side or until barely pink in center. Remove to plate; tent with foil to keep warm.

3 Add apple juice, apple slices, green onion and cherries to skillet; cook 2 to 3 minutes or until apple and green onion are tender.

4 Stir cornstarch into water in small bowl until smooth. Stir into skillet; bring to a boil. Cook and stir about 1 minute or until thickened. Spoon sauce over pork.

Smoked Sausage and Red Pepper Frittata
makes 4 servings

- 4 teaspoons olive oil, divided
- 8 ounces smoked sausage, diced
- 1 red bell pepper, diced
- 1 medium yellow squash, sliced
- ½ cup finely chopped onion
- 4 eggs
- 3 ounces cream cheese
- ½ teaspoon salt
- ¼ teaspoon black pepper
- ¼ cup salsa

1 Heat 2 teaspoons oil in large nonstick skillet over medium-high heat. Add sausage; cook 4 to 5 minutes or until beginning to brown, stirring frequently. Remove to plate.

2 Add remaining 2 teaspoons oil to skillet; heat over medium-high heat. Add bell pepper, squash and onion; cook and stir 4 minutes or until onion is translucent.

3 Meanwhile, combine eggs, cream cheese, salt and black pepper in blender; blend until smooth.

4 Reduce heat to medium-low; stir sausage into vegetable mixture in skillet. Pour egg mixture over sausage and vegetables; cover and cook 10 minutes or until almost set.

5 Remove from heat, let stand uncovered 3 to 4 minutes. Cut into quarters; serve warm or at room temperature with salsa.

Pork Medallions with Marsala
makes 4 servings

½ cup all-purpose flour

½ teaspoon salt

¼ teaspoon black pepper

1 pound pork tenderloin, cut into ½-inch slices

2 tablespoons olive oil

1 clove garlic, chopped

½ cup sweet Marsala wine

2 tablespoons chopped fresh parsley

1 Combine flour, salt and pepper in shallow dish. Coat both sides of pork lightly with flour mixture; shake off excess.

2 Heat oil in large skillet over medium-high heat. Add pork; cook 3 minutes per side or until browned. Remove to plate.

3 Add garlic to skillet; cook and stir over medium heat 1 minute. Stir in wine; cook 1 minute, scraping up browned bits from bottom of skillet. Return pork to skillet; cook 3 minutes or until pork is barely pink in center. Remove to clean plate.

4 Add parsley to skillet; cook 2 to 3 minutes or until sauce is slightly thickened. Serve sauce over pork.

Note

Marsala is a rich, smoky-flavored wine imported from the Mediterranean island of Sicily. This sweet varietal is typically served with dessert but may also be used for cooking.

Pork

Pork and Asparagus Stir-Fry >
makes 4 servings

1 tablespoon vegetable oil

12 ounces pork tenderloin, cut into bite-size pieces

3 tablespoons Chinese black bean sauce

½ teaspoon black pepper

12 ounces asparagus (25 to 30 spears)

2 to 3 tablespoons water

Hot cooked rice (optional)

1 Heat oil in large skillet or wok over medium-high heat. Add pork, black bean sauce and pepper; stir-fry 5 minutes or until pork is browned.

2 Cut asparagus into bite-size pieces. Add asparagus and water to skillet; stir-fry until pork is cooked through and asparagus is crisp-tender, adding additional water if needed to prevent sticking. Serve over rice, if desired.

Pork Chop and Stuffing Skillet
makes 4 servings

4 thin bone-in pork chops (about 4 ounces each)

½ teaspoon salt

¼ teaspoon dried thyme

¼ teaspoon paprika

1 tablespoon olive oil

4 ounces bulk pork sausage

2 cups cornbread stuffing mix

1¼ cups water

1 cup diced green bell pepper

¼ teaspoon poultry seasoning

1 Preheat oven to 350°F. Sprinkle one side of pork chops with salt, thyme and paprika. Heat oil in large ovenproof skillet over medium-high heat. Add pork, seasoned side down; cook 2 minutes. Remove to plate; cover to keep warm.

2 Add sausage to skillet; cook 6 to 8 minutes or until no longer pink, stirring to break up meat. Remove from heat; stir in stuffing mix, water, bell pepper and poultry seasoning just until blended. Place pork, seasoned side up, over stuffing mixture.

3 Cover and bake 15 minutes or until pork is barely pink in center. Let stand 5 minutes before serving.

Seafood

Fish Tacos with Cilantro Cream Sauce
makes 4 servings

½ cup sour cream

¼ cup chopped fresh cilantro

1¼ teaspoons ground cumin, divided

1 pound skinless tilapia, mahi mahi or other firm white fish fillets

1 teaspoon garlic salt

1 teaspoon chipotle hot pepper sauce, divided

1 tablespoon canola or vegetable oil

1 red bell pepper, cut into strips

1 green bell pepper, cut into strips

8 (6-inch) corn tortillas, warmed

4 limes, cut into wedges

1 Combine sour cream, cilantro and ¼ teaspoon cumin in small bowl; mix well. Refrigerate until ready to serve.

2 Cut fish into 1-inch pieces; place in medium bowl. Add remaining 1 teaspoon cumin, garlic salt and ½ teaspoon hot pepper sauce; toss gently to coat.

3 Heat oil in large nonstick skillet over medium heat. Add fish; cook 1¼ to 2 minutes per side or just until fish is opaque in center. Remove to plate. Add bell peppers to skillet; cook 6 to 8 minutes or until tender, stirring occasionally.

4 Return fish to skillet with remaining ½ teaspoon hot pepper sauce; cook and stir just until heated through. Serve in tortillas with sauce and lime wedges.

Pan-Seared Sole with Lemon-Butter Caper Sauce

makes 2 servings

¼ cup all-purpose flour

½ teaspoon plus
⅛ teaspoon salt,
divided

¼ teaspoon black pepper

1 pound Dover sole fillets

2 tablespoons vegetable
oil

3 tablespoons butter

2 tablespoons lemon juice

2 teaspoons capers,
rinsed, drained
and chopped

2 tablespoons finely
chopped fresh chives

1 Combine flour, ½ teaspoon salt and pepper in shallow dish or pie plate. Coat fish with flour mixture, shaking off excess.

2 Heat oil in large nonstick skillet over medium heat. Add half of fillets; cook 2 to 3 minutes per side or until golden brown. Remove to plate; tent with foil to keep warm. Repeat with remaining fillets.

3 Wipe out skillet with paper towels. Add butter and remaining ⅛ teaspoon salt; cook 20 to 30 seconds or until melted and lightly browned. Remove from heat; stir in lemon juice and capers.

4 Drizzle sauce over fish; sprinkle with chives. Serve immediately.

Blackened Shrimp with Tomatoes
makes 4 servings

1½ teaspoons paprika

1 teaspoon Italian seasoning

½ teaspoon garlic powder

¼ teaspoon salt

¼ teaspoon black pepper

8 ounces small raw shrimp, peeled (about 24)

1 tablespoon canola oil

1½ cups halved grape tomatoes

½ cup sliced onion, separated into rings

Lime wedges (optional)

1 Combine paprika, Italian seasoning, garlic powder, salt and pepper in small bowl; mix well. Pour into large resealable food storage bag. Add shrimp; seal bag and shake to coat.

2 Heat oil in large skillet over medium-high heat. Add shrimp; cook 4 minutes or until shrimp are pink and opaque, turning occasionally.

3 Add tomatoes and onion to skillet; cook 2 minutes or until tomatoes are heated through and onion is softened. Serve with lime wedges, if desired.

Orange-Glazed Salmon
makes 4 servings

Glaze

2 **tablespoons orange juice**

2 **tablespoons soy sauce**

1 **tablespoon honey**

¾ **teaspoon grated fresh ginger**

½ **teaspoon rice wine vinegar**

¼ **teaspoon toasted sesame oil**

Salmon

4 **salmon fillets (about 6 ounces each)**

½ **teaspoon salt**

¼ **teaspoon black pepper**

1 **tablespoon olive oil**

1 For glaze, whisk orange juice, soy sauce, honey, ginger, vinegar and sesame oil in small bowl until well blended.

2 Season salmon with salt and pepper. Heat olive oil in large nonstick skillet over medium-high heat. Place fish skin side up in skillet; brush with glaze. Cook 4 minutes. Carefully turn fish; brush with some of remaining glaze. Cook 4 minutes or just until fish begins to flake when tested with fork. Transfer to plate; tent with foil to keep warm.

3 Meanwhile, place remaining glaze in small saucepan; cook and stir until thickened and reduced to about 2 tablespoons. Serve over salmon.

Adriatic-Style Halibut
makes 4 servings

1 large tomato, seeded and diced (about 1¼ cups)

⅓ cup coarsely sliced pitted kalamata olives

1 clove garlic, minced

4 skinless halibut or red snapper fillets (about 6 ounces each)

¾ teaspoon coarse salt

¼ teaspoon black pepper

1 tablespoon olive oil

¼ cup dry white wine or vermouth

2 tablespoons chopped fresh basil or Italian parsley

1 Preheat oven to 200°F. Combine tomato, olives and garlic in small bowl; mix well.

2 Season fish with ¾ teaspoon salt and ¼ teaspoon pepper. Heat oil in large nonstick skillet over medium heat. Add fish; cook 4 to 5 minutes per side or just until fish is opaque in center. Transfer to platter or plate; keep warm in oven.

3 Add wine to skillet; cook over high heat until reduced by half. Add tomato mixture; cook and stir 1 to 2 minutes or until heated through. Season with additional salt and pepper. Spoon tomato mixture over fish; sprinkle with basil.

Thai Shrimp Curry
makes 4 servings

1 can (14 ounces) unsweetened coconut milk, divided

1 teaspoon Thai red curry paste

⅓ cup water

1 tablespoon brown sugar

1 tablespoon fish sauce

Peel of 1 lime, finely chopped

1 pound large raw shrimp, peeled and deveined

½ cup fresh basil leaves, thinly sliced

Hot cooked jasmine rice

Fresh pineapple wedges (optional)

½ cup unsalted peanuts (optional)

1 Pour half of coconut milk into large skillet; bring to a boil over medium heat, stirring occasionally. Cook 5 to 6 minutes; oil may start to rise to surface. Add curry paste; cook and stir 2 minutes.

2 Combine remaining coconut milk and water; add to skillet with brown sugar, fish sauce and lime peel. Cook over medium-low heat 10 to 15 minutes or until sauce thickens slightly.

3 Stir in shrimp and basil. Reduce heat to low; cook 3 to 5 minutes or until shrimp turn pink and opaque. Serve over rice; garnish with pineapple and peanuts.

Roasted Dill Scrod with Asparagus
makes 4 servings

1 **bunch (12 ounces) asparagus spears, ends trimmed**

1 **teaspoon olive oil**

4 **scrod or cod fillets (about 5 ounces each)**

1 **tablespoon lemon juice**

1 **teaspoon dried dill weed**

½ **teaspoon salt**

¼ **teaspoon black pepper**

Paprika (optional)

1 Preheat oven to 425°F.

2 Place asparagus in 13×9-inch baking dish; drizzle with oil. Roll asparagus to coat lightly with oil; push to edges of dish, stacking asparagus into two layers.

3 Arrange fish fillets in center of baking dish; drizzle with lemon juice. Combine dill weed, salt and pepper in small bowl; sprinkle over fish and asparagus. Sprinkle with paprika, if desired.

4 Roast 15 to 17 minutes or until asparagus is crisp-tender and fish is opaque in center and begins to flake when tested with fork.

Pecan Catfish with Cranberry Compote
makes 4 servings

Cranberry Compote
(recipe follows)

2 tablespoons butter,
   divided

1½ cups pecans

2 tablespoons
   all-purpose flour

1 egg

2 tablespoons water

Salt and black pepper

4 catfish fillets (about
   5 ounces each)

1 Preheat oven to 425°F. Prepare Cranberry Compote.

2 Melt 1 tablespoon butter; place in 13×9-inch baking pan, tilting pan to coat evenly. Combine pecans and flour in food processor; pulse just until nuts are finely chopped.

3 Place pecan mixture in shallow dish. Whisk egg and water in another shallow dish. Season both sides of each fillet with salt and pepper. Dip fish in egg mixture, letting excess drip back into dish. Coat fish with pecan mixture, pressing to lightly to adhere. Place in prepared pan; dot with remaining 1 tablespoon butter.

4 Bake 15 to 20 minutes or until fish begins to flake when tested with fork. Serve with Cranberry Compote.

Cranberry Compote
makes about 3 cups

1 package (12 ounces)
   fresh cranberries

¾ cup water

⅔ cup sugar

¼ cup orange juice

2 teaspoons grated
   fresh ginger

¼ teaspoon Chinese
   five-spice powder

⅛ teaspoon salt

1 teaspoon butter

1 Combine cranberries, water, sugar, orange juice, ginger, five-spice powder and salt in large saucepan; cook over medium-high heat 10 minutes or until berries begin to pop, stirring occasionally. Reduce heat to medium; cook and stir 5 minutes or until sauce is thickened.

2 Remove from heat; stir in butter until melted. Let stand 10 minutes. (Compote can be made up to 1 week in advance and stored in the refrigerator.)

Shrimp and Veggie Skillet
makes 4 servings

¼ cup soy sauce

2 tablespoons lime juice

1 tablespoon sesame oil

1 teaspoon grated
   fresh ginger

⅛ teaspoon red pepper
   flakes

1 tablespoon vegetable
   oil, divided

8 ounces raw shrimp,
   peeled, deveined
   and patted dry

2 medium zucchini, cut in
   half lengthwise and
   thinly sliced

6 green onions, trimmed
   and halved lengthwise

1 cup grape tomatoes

1 Whisk soy sauce, lime juice, sesame oil, ginger and red pepper flakes in small bowl until well blended.

2 Heat half of vegetable oil in large nonstick skillet over medium-high heat. Add shrimp; cook and stir 3 minutes or until shrimp are opaque. Remove to large bowl.

3 Add remaining oil to skillet; heat over medium-high heat. Add zucchini; cook and stir 4 to 6 minutes or until crisp-tender. Add green onions and tomatoes; cook 1 to 2 minutes. Add shrimp, cook 1 minute. Return to large bowl.

4 Add soy sauce mixture to skillet; bring to a boil. Remove from heat. Add shrimp and vegetables to skillet; toss gently to coat.

Roasted Salmon with Potatoes and Onions
makes 6 servings

¼ cup chicken broth

1 tablespoon olive oil

1½ pounds small new potatoes, cut into halves

1 medium red onion, cut into ¼-inch-thick wedges

6 salmon fillets (4 ounces each)

¾ teaspoon salt

½ teaspoon black pepper

Fresh tarragon or dill sprigs (optional)

1 Preheat oven to 400°F. Spray large shallow roasting pan or baking sheet with nonstick cooking spray.

2 Combine broth and oil in small bowl. Combine potatoes and half of broth mixture in prepared pan; toss to coat. Roast 20 minutes.

3 Add onion and remaining broth mixture to pan; stir to coat. Push vegetables to edges of pan; place fish in center. Sprinkle fish and vegetables with salt and pepper; roast 10 to 15 minutes or until fish is opaque in center and vegetables are tender. Garnish with tarragon.

Meatless

Southwestern Flatbread with Black Beans and Corn
makes 4 servings

2 oval flatbreads (about 11×7 inches)

¼ cup prepared green chile enchilada sauce

2 cups (8 ounces) shredded Monterey Jack cheese

1 can (about 15 ounces) black beans, rinsed and drained

1 cup frozen corn, thawed

½ cup finely chopped red onion

1 teaspoon olive oil

½ teaspoon kosher salt

1 avocado, diced

2 tablespoons fresh chopped cilantro

Lime wedges (optional)

1 Preheat oven to 425°F. Place wire rack on large baking sheet; place flatbreads on rack.

2 Spread enchilada sauce over flatbreads; sprinkle with cheese. Combine beans, corn, onion, oil and salt in medium bowl; mix well. Spread mixture evenly over cheese.

3 Bake 12 minutes or until flatbreads are golden and crisp and cheese is melted.

4 Sprinkle avocado and cilantro over flatbreads; serve with lime wedges, if desired.

Pumpkin Curry
makes 4 servings

1 tablespoon vegetable oil

1 package (14 ounces) firm tofu, drained, patted dry and cut into 1-inch cubes

¼ cup Thai red curry paste

2 cloves garlic, minced

1 can (15 ounces) pure pumpkin

1 can (about 13 ounces) coconut milk

1 cup vegetable broth or water

1½ teaspoons salt

1 teaspoon sriracha sauce

4 cups cut-up fresh vegetables (broccoli, cauliflower, red bell pepper and/or sweet potato)

½ cup peas

Hot cooked rice

¼ cup shredded fresh basil (optional)

1 Heat oil in large skillet or wok over high heat. Add tofu; cook and stir 5 minutes or until lightly browned. Add curry paste and garlic; cook and stir 1 minute or until tofu is coated.

2 Add pumpkin, coconut milk, broth, salt and sriracha; bring to a boil. Stir in vegetables. Reduce heat to medium; cover and simmer 20 minutes or until vegetables are tender.

3 Stir in peas; cook 1 minute or until heated through. Serve with rice; top with basil, if desired.

Frittata Rustica
makes 2 servings

4 ounces cremini mushrooms, stems trimmed, cut into thirds

1 tablespoon olive oil, divided

½ teaspoon plus ⅛ teaspoon salt, divided

½ cup chopped onion

1 cup packed chopped stemmed lacinato kale

½ cup halved grape tomatoes

4 eggs

½ teaspoon Italian seasoning

Black pepper

⅓ cup shredded mozzarella cheese

1 tablespoon shredded Parmesan cheese

Chopped fresh parsley (optional)

1 Preheat oven to 400°F. Spread mushrooms on small baking sheet; drizzle with 1 teaspoon oil and sprinkle with ⅛ teaspoon salt. Roast 15 to 20 minutes or until well browned and tender.

2 Heat remaining 2 teaspoons oil in small (6- to 8-inch) ovenproof nonstick skillet over medium heat. Add onion; cook and stir 5 minutes or until soft. Add kale and ¼ teaspoon salt; cook and stir 10 minutes or until kale is tender. Add tomatoes; cook and stir 3 minutes or until tomatoes are soft. Stir in mushrooms.

3 Preheat broiler. Beat eggs, remaining ¼ teaspoon salt, Italian seasoning and pepper in small bowl until well blended.

4 Pour egg mixture over vegetables in skillet; stir gently to mix. Cook 3 minutes or until eggs are set around edge, lifting edge to allow uncooked portion to flow underneath. Sprinkle with mozzarella and Parmesan.

5 Broil 3 minutes or until eggs are set and cheese is browned. Cut into four wedges. Garnish with parsley.

Chickpea Tikka Masala
makes 4 servings

1 tablespoon olive oil

1 onion, chopped

3 cloves garlic, minced

1 tablespoon minced fresh ginger or ginger paste

1 tablespoon garam masala

1 teaspoon ground cumin

1 teaspoon ground coriander

1 teaspoon salt

¼ teaspoon ground red pepper

2 cans (about 15 ounces each) chickpeas, drained

1 can (28 ounces) crushed tomatoes

1 can (about 13 ounces) coconut milk

1 package (about 12 ounces) firm silken tofu, drained and cut into 1-inch cubes

Hot cooked rice

Chopped fresh cilantro (optional)

1 Heat oil in large saucepan over medium-high heat. Add onion; cook and stir 5 minutes or until translucent. Add garlic, ginger, garam masala, cumin, coriander, salt and red pepper; cook and stir 1 minute.

2 Stir in chickpeas, tomatoes and coconut milk. Reduce heat to medium; simmer, uncovered, 30 minutes or until sauce is thickened and chickpeas have softened slightly.

3 Gently stir in tofu; cook 7 to 10 minutes or until tofu is heated through. Serve over rice; garnish with cilantro.

Sticky Tofu
makes 4 servings

1 cup uncooked brown rice or medium-grain white rice

¼ cup ketchup

3 tablespoons soy sauce

2 tablespoons packed brown sugar

2 cloves garlic, minced

1 package (14 to 16 ounces) firm or extra firm tofu, drained

Salt and black pepper

3 tablespoons cornstarch

1 tablespoon vegetable oil

1 head bok choy, sliced lengthwise ½-inch thick, then crosswise into thin slices

Hot cooked rice

1 Cook rice according to package directions; keep warm.

2 Combine ketchup, soy sauce, brown sugar and garlic in medium bowl; mix well.

3 Cut tofu into cubes; pat dry with paper towels. Season with salt and pepper. Place cornstarch in large bowl; add tofu and toss gently to coat.

4 Heat oil in large skillet over medium-high heat. Add tofu; cook 5 minutes or until lightly browned, stirring occasionally. Add bok choy; cook and stir 5 minutes. Add sauce; cook and stir 5 to 7 minutes or until sauce is thickened and slightly caramelized. Serve over rice.

Black Bean and Rice
Stuffed Poblano Peppers
makes 4 servings

4 poblano peppers

1 can (about 15 ounces) black beans, rinsed and drained

1 cup cooked brown rice

⅔ cup chunky salsa

⅔ cup shredded Cheddar cheese or pepper-jack cheese, divided

½ teaspoon salt

1 Preheat oven to 375°F. Spray shallow baking pan with nonstick cooking spray.

2 Cut thin slice from one side of each pepper. Chop pepper slices; set aside.

3 Bring medium saucepan of water to a boil. Add whole peppers; cook 6 minutes. Drain and rinse with cold water. Remove and discard seeds and membranes.

4 Combine beans, rice, salsa, ½ cup cheese, chopped pepper and salt in small bowl; mix well. Spoon into peppers, mounding mixture. Place peppers in prepared pan; cover with foil.

5 Bake 12 to 15 minutes or until heated through. Sprinkle with remaining cheese; bake 2 minutes or until cheese is melted.

Green Curry with Tofu
makes 2 to 4 servings

1 tablespoon vegetable oil

1 onion, chopped

1 package (14 ounces) firm tofu, drained and cut into 1-inch cubes

⅓ cup Thai green curry paste

1 can (about 13 ounces) coconut milk

1 broccoli crown (about 8 ounces), cut into florets

1 cup cut green beans (1-inch pieces)

½ teaspoon salt

Hot cooked rice or rice noodles

1 Heat oil in large skillet or wok over high heat. Add onion; cook and stir 5 minutes or until soft and lightly browned.

2 Add tofu and curry paste; cook and stir 2 minutes or until curry is fragrant and tofu is coated. Add coconut milk; bring to a boil.

3 Stir in broccoli and green beans; cook over low heat 20 minutes or until vegetables are tender and sauce is thickened, stirring frequently. Season with salt. Serve with rice.

Shortcut Spanish Tortilla
makes 4 to 6 servings

2 tablespoons olive oil

1 medium onion, cut in half and thinly sliced

10 eggs

½ teaspoon salt

⅛ teaspoon black pepper

5 ounces potato chips (use plain thin chips, not kettle), lightly crushed

Chopped fresh chives or parsley (optional)

1 Preheat oven to 350°F. Spray 8-inch round cake pan with nonstick cooking spray.

2 Heat oil in medium skillet over medium-high heat. Add onion; cook and stir 5 minutes or until onion is softened and beginning to brown. Remove from heat; set aside to cool 5 minutes.

3 Meanwhile, beat eggs, salt and pepper in medium bowl until blended. Add potato chips; fold in gently until all chips are coated. Let stand 5 minutes to soften. Stir in onion until well blended. Pour egg mixture into prepared pan; smooth top.

4 Bake 25 minutes or until toothpick inserted into center comes out clean. Remove to wire rack; cool 5 minutes. Loosen tortilla from side of pan, if necessary. Invert tortilla onto plate; invert again onto large serving plate or cutting board. Garnish with chives.

Portobello Provolone Panini
makes 4 servings

6 to 8 ounces sliced portobello mushrooms

⅓ cup plus 1 tablespoon olive oil, divided

3 tablespoons balsamic vinegar

1 clove garlic, minced

½ teaspoon salt

¼ teaspoon black pepper

1 loaf (16 ounces) ciabatta or Italian bread

8 ounces sliced provolone cheese

¼ cup chopped fresh basil

8 ounces plum tomatoes, thinly sliced

3 tablespoons whole grain Dijon mustard

1 Combine mushrooms, ⅓ cup oil, vinegar, garlic, salt and pepper in large bowl; mix well. Let stand 15 minutes, turning frequently. (Mushrooms may be prepared up to 24 hours in advance; cover and refrigerate.)

2 Preheat indoor grill or grill pan. Brush both sides of bread with remaining 1 tablespoon oil; cut bread in half lengthwise.

3 Arrange mushrooms evenly over bottom half of bread; drizzle with some of remaining marinade. Top with cheese, basil and tomatoes. Spread mustard over cut side of remaining half of bread; place over tomatoes. Cut sandwich into four equal pieces.

4 Grill sandwiches 8 minutes or until cheese is melted and bread is golden brown. Wrap sandwiches tightly in foil to keep warm or serve at room temperature.

Red Lentil and Chickpea Stew
makes 6 servings

1 tablespoon olive oil

1 onion, chopped

3 cloves garlic, minced

2 tablespoons minced fresh ginger

1 tablespoon curry powder

2 teaspoons ground turmeric

1½ teaspoons salt

⅛ teaspoon ground red pepper

1 container (32 ounces) vegetable broth

1¼ cups uncooked red lentils (8 ounces)

1 can (about 15 ounces) chickpeas, rinsed and drained

1 can (14 ounces) coconut milk

1 package (about 5 ounces) baby spinach

Large coconut flakes and chopped fresh cilantro (optional)

1 Heat oil in large saucepan over medium-high heat. Add onion; cook and stir 5 minutes or until softened. Add garlic, ginger, curry powder, turmeric, salt and red pepper; cook and stir 1 minute.

2 Stir in broth; bring to a boil. Stir in lentils; cook 15 minutes.

3 Stir in chickpeas and coconut milk; cook 5 to 10 minutes or until lentils are tender, chickpeas are heated through and stew is slightly thickened. Add spinach; cook and stir 2 to 3 minutes or just until spinach is wilted. Garnish with coconut and cilantro.

Pasta

Spicy Chicken Rigatoni
makes 4 servings

2 tablespoons olive oil

2 cloves garlic, minced

½ teaspoon red pepper flakes

½ teaspoon black pepper

8 ounces boneless skinless chicken breasts, cut into thin strips

1 cup marinara sauce

¾ cup Alfredo sauce

1 package (16 ounces) mezzo rigatoni, rigatoni or penne pasta, cooked until al dente

¾ cup frozen peas, thawed

Grated Parmesan cheese (optional)

1 Heat oil in large saucepan over medium-high heat. Add garlic, red pepper flakes and black pepper; cook and stir 1 minute. Add chicken; cook and stir 4 minutes or until cooked through.

2 Add marinara sauce and Alfredo sauce; stir until blended. Reduce heat to medium-low; cook 10 minutes, stirring occasionally.

3 Add pasta and peas; stir gently to coat. Cook 2 minutes or until heated through. Sprinkle with cheese, if desired.

Sesame Noodles
makes 6 to 8 servings

1 package (16 ounces) uncooked spaghetti

6 tablespoons soy sauce

5 tablespoons toasted sesame oil

3 tablespoons sugar

3 tablespoons rice vinegar

2 tablespoons vegetable oil

3 cloves garlic, minced

1 teaspoon grated fresh ginger

½ teaspoon sriracha

2 green onions, sliced

1 red bell pepper

1 cucumber

1 carrot

Sesame seeds (optional)

1 Cook pasta in large saucepan of boiling salted water according to package directions for al dente. Drain pasta, reserving 1 tablespoon pasta cooking water.

2 Whisk soy sauce, sesame oil, sugar, vinegar, vegetable oil, garlic, ginger, sriracha and reserved pasta water in large bowl. Stir in pasta and green onions. Let stand at least 30 minutes until pasta has cooled to room temperature and most of sauce is absorbed, stirring occasionally.

3 Meanwhile, cut bell pepper into thin strips. Peel cucumber and carrot and shred with julienne peeler into long strands, or cut into thin strips. Stir into pasta. Serve at room temperature or refrigerate until ready to serve. Top with sesame seeds, if desired.

Orecchiette with Sausage and Broccoli Rabe
makes 4 to 6 servings

1 tablespoon olive oil

12 ounces bulk mild Italian sausage

3 cloves garlic, minced

¼ teaspoon red pepper flakes

4 cups chicken broth, divided

¾ teaspoon salt

1 package (16 ounces) uncooked orecchiette pasta

1 bunch broccoli rabe (about 1 pound), tough stems removed, cut into 2-inch-long pieces

¾ cup grated Parmesan cheese, divided

Juice of 1 lemon

1 Heat oil in large saucepan or Dutch oven over medium-high heat. Add sausage; cook about 8 minutes or until browned, stirring to break up meat. Add garlic and red pepper flakes; cook and stir 1 minute. Add 2 tablespoons broth; cook 1 minute, scraping up browned bits from bottom of saucepan.

2 Stir in remaining broth and salt; bring to a boil. Add pasta, stirring to separate pieces as much as possible. (Orecchiette pasta often sticks together in stacks in the package and during cooking.) Reduce heat to medium; cover and cook 10 minutes, stirring occasionally to prevent pasta from sticking.

3 Add broccoli rabe to saucepan; stir to wilt and blend with pasta. Cover and cook 4 minutes or until pasta is tender and liquid is absorbed, stirring occasionally.

4 Stir in ½ cup cheese and lemon juice; mix well. Serve immediately with remaining cheese.

Three-Cheese Macaroni and Quinoa
makes 4 servings

4 tablespoons (½ stick) butter, divided

½ cup panko bread crumbs

2 quarts water

1 teaspoon salt, divided

6 ounces uncooked whole grain elbow macaroni (1½ cups)

½ cup uncooked quinoa, preferably white grain

2 tablespoons all-purpose flour

1 cup milk

1 cup (4 ounces) shredded sharp Cheddar cheese

1 cup (4 ounces) shredded Monterey Jack cheese

¼ cup grated Parmesan cheese

Optional toppings: finely chopped green onion, chopped fresh parsley and/or diced fresh tomato

1 Melt 2 tablespoons butter in large saucepan over medium heat. Add panko; cook and stir 1 to 2 minutes or until golden. Remove to small bowl. Wipe out saucepan with paper towel.

2 Combine water and ½ teaspoon salt in same saucepan; bring to a boil over high heat. Stir in macaroni and quinoa; boil 10 minutes. Drain in fine-mesh strainer. Transfer to large serving bowl; cover to keep warm.

3 Melt remaining 2 tablespoons butter in same saucepan over medium heat. Whisk in flour; cook and stir 1 minute. Gradually whisk in milk and remaining ½ teaspoon salt; cook and stir 5 minutes or until very thick. Stir in Cheddar and Monterey Jack until melted. Pour over macaroni mixture; stir gently until blended.

4 Top with Parmesan and panko. Garnish as desired.

Note

For a spicy flavor, substitute pepper Jack cheese for the Monterey Jack.

Meaty Sausage Spaghetti
makes 6 to 8 servings

1 tablespoon olive oil

1 cup chopped onion

2 cloves garlic, minced

1 package (20 ounces) bulk Italian sausage

1 cup chopped yellow, red and/or green bell peppers

1 can (about 14 ounces) crushed tomatoes

1 can (about 14 ounces) diced tomatoes

2½ teaspoons salt

2 teaspoons dried basil

1 teaspoon dried oregano

¼ teaspoon black pepper

2½ to 3 cups water, divided

1 package (16 ounces) uncooked spaghetti, broken in half

Grated Parmesan cheese

1 Heat oil in large saucepan or Dutch oven over medium-high heat. Add onion and garlic; cook and stir 3 minutes or until onion is softened. Add sausage; cook until browned, stirring to break up meat. Drain fat. Add bell peppers; cook and stir 2 minutes. Add crushed tomatoes, diced tomatoes, salt, basil, oregano and pepper; mix well.

2 Add pasta to saucepan; stir gently to allow some liquid to get between strands of spaghetti to prevent sticking. Add 2½ cups water; bring to a boil. Reduce heat to medium; cover and cook 15 minutes, stirring occasionally.

3 Uncover; add additional water if pasta seems dry. Test for doneness; continue to cook 2 to 3 minutes or until pasta reaches desired doneness, stirring frequently. Season with additional salt and pepper. Serve immediately with cheese.

Note

You can use 1 pound of ground beef, ground pork, meatloaf mix or even plant-based meat substitute in place of the sausage.

Vegetable Penne Italiano
makes 4 servings

1 tablespoon olive oil

1 red bell pepper, cut into ½-inch pieces

1 green bell pepper, cut into ½-inch pieces

1 medium sweet onion, halved and thinly sliced

3 cloves garlic, minced

2 tablespoons tomato paste

2 teaspoons salt

1 teaspoon sugar

1 teaspoon Italian seasoning

¼ teaspoon black pepper

1 can (28 ounces) Italian plum tomatoes, undrained, chopped

8 ounces uncooked penne pasta

Grated Parmesan cheese

Chopped fresh basil

1 Heat oil in large skillet over medium-high heat. Add bell peppers, onion and garlic; cook 8 minutes or until vegetables are crisp-tender, stirring occasionally.

2 Add tomato paste, salt, sugar, Italian seasoning and black pepper; cook and stir 1 minute. Stir in tomatoes with juice. Reduce heat to medium-low; cook 15 minutes or until vegetables are tender and sauce is thickened.

3 Meanwhile, cook pasta in large saucepan of salted boiling water according to package directions until al dente. Drain and return to saucepan.

4 Pour sauce over pasta; stir gently to coat. Divide among four serving bowls; top with cheese and basil.

Lo Mein Noodles with Shrimp
makes 4 servings

- 12 ounces Chinese-style thin egg noodles
- 2 teaspoons sesame oil
- 1½ tablespoons oyster sauce
- 1½ tablespoons soy sauce
- ½ teaspoon sugar
- ¼ teaspoon salt
- ¼ teaspoon white or black pepper
- 2 tablespoons vegetable oil
- 1 teaspoon minced fresh ginger
- 1 clove garlic, minced
- 8 ounces medium shrimp, peeled and deveined
- 2 green onions, cut into 1-inch pieces
- ¼ cup fresh chives, cut into 1-inch pieces
- 1 tablespoon dry sherry
- 8 ounces bean sprouts

1 Cook noodles in boiling water according to package directions 2 to 3 minutes or until tender but still firm. Drain noodles; rinse under cold water and drain.

2 Combine noodles and sesame oil in large bowl; stir to coat.

3 Whisk oyster sauce, soy sauce, sugar, salt and pepper in small bowl until well blended.

4 Heat vegetable oil in large skillet or wok over high heat. Add ginger and garlic; stir-fry 10 seconds. Add shrimp; stir-fry about 1 minute or until shrimp begin to turn pink. Add green onions, chives and sherry; stir-fry 15 seconds or until chives begin to wilt. Add half of bean sprouts; stir-fry 15 seconds. Add remaining bean sprouts; stir-fry 15 seconds.

5 Add oyster sauce mixture and noodles; cook and stir about 2 minutes or until heated through.

Mediterranean Orzo and Vegetable Pilaf
makes 4 servings

½ cup plus 2 tablespoons (4 ounces) uncooked orzo pasta

1 tablespoon olive oil

1 small onion, diced

2 cloves garlic, minced

1 zucchini, diced

½ cup chicken broth

1 can (about 14 ounces) artichoke hearts, drained and quartered

1 medium tomato, chopped

½ teaspoon dried oregano

½ teaspoon salt

¼ teaspoon black pepper

½ cup (2 ounces) crumbled feta cheese

Sliced black olives (optional)

1 Cook pasta according to package directions; drain.

2 Meanwhile, heat oil in large skillet over medium heat. Add onion; cook and stir 5 minutes or until translucent. Add garlic; cook and stir 1 minute. Reduce heat to low. Stir in zucchini and broth; cook 5 minutes or until zucchini is crisp-tender.

3 Add cooked pasta, artichokes, tomato, oregano, salt and pepper; cook and stir 1 minute or until heated through. Top with cheese and olives, if desired.

Fettuccine alla Carbonara
makes 4 servings

12 ounces uncooked
fettuccine

4 ounces pancetta or
bacon, cut into
½-inch pieces

3 cloves garlic, cut
into halves

¼ cup dry white wine

⅓ cup whipping cream

1 egg

1 egg yolk

⅔ cup grated Parmesan
cheese, divided

Dash white pepper

1 Cook pasta according to package directions. Drain and return to saucepan; cover to keep warm.

2 Cook and stir pancetta and garlic in large skillet over medium-low heat 4 minutes or until lightly browned. Drain off all but 2 tablespoons drippings from skillet.

3 Add wine to skillet; cook over medium heat 3 minutes or until almost evaporated. Add cream; cook and stir 2 minutes. Remove from heat; discard garlic.

4 Whisk egg and egg yolk in top of double boiler; place over simmering water, adjusting heat to maintain simmer. Whisk ⅓ cup cheese and pepper into egg mixture; cook and stir until thickened.

5 Pour pancetta mixture over pasta; stir to coat. Cook over medium-low heat until heated through. Add egg mixture; stir to coat. Serve with remaining ⅓ cup cheese.

Szechuan Cold Noodles
makes 4 servings

- 8 ounces uncooked vermicelli, broken in half, or Chinese egg noodles
- 3 tablespoons rice vinegar
- 3 tablespoons soy sauce
- 2 tablespoons peanut or vegetable oil
- 1 clove garlic, minced
- 1 teaspoon minced fresh ginger
- 1 teaspoon dark sesame oil
- ½ teaspoon crushed Szechuan peppercorns or red pepper flakes
- ¼ cup coarsely chopped fresh cilantro (optional)
- ¼ cup chopped peanuts

1 Cook pasta according to package directions; drain.

2 Whisk vinegar, soy sauce, peanut oil, garlic, ginger, sesame oil, if desired, and peppercorns in large bowl until well blended.

3 Add hot pasta; stir to coat. Sprinkle with cilantro, if desired, and peanuts. Serve at room temperature or chilled.

Szechuan Vegetable Noodles

Add 1 cup chopped peeled cucumber, ½ cup chopped red bell pepper, ½ cup sliced green onions and an additional 1 tablespoon soy sauce.

Vegetables & Sides

Sweet Potato Fries
makes 2 servings

1 large sweet potato
(about 8 ounces)

1 tablespoon olive oil

¼ teaspoon coarse salt

¼ teaspoon black pepper

¼ teaspoon ground
red pepper

Honey or maple syrup
(optional)

1 Preheat oven to 425°F. Spray baking sheet with nonstick cooking spray.

2 Peel sweet potato; cut lengthwise into long spears. Combine sweet potatoes, oil, salt, black pepper and red pepper on prepared baking sheet. Spread in single layer not touching.

3 Bake 20 to 30 minutes or until lightly browned, turning halfway through cooking time. Serve with honey, if desired.

Roasted Mushrooms with Shallots >
makes 4 servings

1 pound cremini mushrooms, halved

½ cup sliced shallots

1 tablespoon olive oil

½ teaspoon coarse salt

½ teaspoon dried rosemary

¼ teaspoon black pepper

Fresh rosemary sprigs (optional)

1 Preheat oven to 400°F.

2 Combine mushrooms and shallots on large baking sheet. Combine oil, salt, dried rosemary and pepper in small bowl; mix well. Drizzle over vegetables; toss to coat. Spread in single layer on baking sheet.

3 Roast 15 to 18 minutes or until mushrooms are browned and tender. Garnish with fresh rosemary.

Creamy Parmesan Spinach
makes 4 to 6 servings

2 tablespoons butter, divided

1 cup finely chopped onion

2 packages (9 ounces each) fresh spinach, divided

3 ounces cream cheese, cut into pieces

½ teaspoon salt

½ teaspoon garlic powder

¼ teaspoon ground nutmeg

¼ teaspoon black pepper

¼ cup grated Parmesan cheese

1 Melt 1 tablespoon butter in large skillet over medium-high heat. Add onion; cook and stir 4 minutes or until translucent.

2 Add one package of spinach; cook and stir 2 minutes or just until wilted. Transfer spinach mixture to medium bowl. Repeat with remaining 1 tablespoon butter and spinach.

3 Return spinach to skillet. Add cream cheese, salt, garlic powder, nutmeg and pepper; cook and stir until cream cheese has completely melted. Sprinkle with Parmesan just before serving.

Tip

For a thinner consistency, stir in 2 to 3 tablespoons milk before adding the Parmesan.

Smashed Potatoes >
makes 4 servings

4 medium russet potatoes
(about 1½ pounds),
peeled and cut into
¼-inch cubes

⅓ cup milk

2 tablespoons sour cream

1 tablespoon minced
onion

½ teaspoon salt

¼ teaspoon black pepper

⅛ teaspoon garlic powder
(optional)

Chopped fresh chives
or French fried onions
(optional)

1 Bring large saucepan of lightly salted water to
a boil over medium-high heat. Add potatoes;
cook 15 to 20 minutes or until fork-tender.
Drain and return to saucepan.

2 Slightly mash potatoes. Stir in milk, sour cream,
minced onion, salt, pepper and garlic powder,
if desired. Mash until desired texture is reached,
leaving potatoes chunky. Cook over low heat
5 minutes or until heated through, stirring
occasionally. Garnish with chives.

Kale with Lemon and Garlic
makes 6 to 8 servings

2 bunches kale or Swiss
chard (1 to 1¼ pounds)

1 tablespoon olive oil

3 cloves garlic, minced

½ cup chicken or
vegetable broth

½ teaspoon salt

¼ teaspoon black pepper

1 lemon, cut into 8 wedges

1 Trim tough stems from kale; stack and thinly
slice leaves.

2 Heat oil in large saucepan over medium heat.
Add garlic; cook 3 minutes, stirring occasionally.
Add chopped kale and broth; cover and cook
7 minutes. Stir kale; cover and cook over
medium-low heat 8 to 10 minutes or until
tender.

3 Stir in salt and pepper. Squeeze wedge of
lemon over each serving.

Roasted Curried Cauliflower and Brussels Sprouts ›
makes 10 servings

- 2 pounds cauliflower florets
- 12 ounces Brussels sprouts, cleaned and cut in half lengthwise
- ⅓ cup olive oil
- ½ teaspoon salt
- ½ teaspoon black pepper
- 2½ tablespoons curry powder
- ½ cup chopped fresh cilantro

1 Preheat oven to 400°F. Line baking sheet with foil.

2 Combine cauliflower, Brussels sprouts and oil in large bowl; toss to coat. Sprinkle with salt, pepper and curry powder; toss to coat. Spread vegetables in single layer on prepared baking sheet.

3 Roast 20 to 25 minutes or until golden brown, stirring after 15 minutes. Add cilantro; stir until blended.

Balsamic Butternut Squash
makes 4 servings

- 3 tablespoons olive oil
- 2 tablespoons thinly sliced fresh sage (about 6 large leaves), divided
- 1 medium butternut squash, peeled and cut into 1-inch pieces (4 to 5 cups)
- ½ small red onion, cut in half and cut into ¼-inch slices
- 1 teaspoon salt, divided
- 2½ tablespoons balsamic vinegar
- ¼ teaspoon black pepper

1 Heat oil in large skillet over medium-high heat. Add 1 tablespoon sage; cook and stir 3 minutes. Add squash, onion and ½ teaspoon salt; cook 6 minutes, stirring occasionally. Reduce heat to medium; cook 15 minutes without stirring.

2 Stir in vinegar, remaining ½ teaspoon salt and pepper; cook 10 minutes or until squash is tender, stirring occasionally. Stir in remaining 1 tablespoon sage; cook 1 minute.

Green Beans with Garlic-Cilantro Butter >
makes 4 to 6 servings

1½ pounds green beans, trimmed

3 tablespoons butter

1 red bell pepper, cut into thin strips

½ sweet onion, halved and thinly sliced

2 teaspoons minced garlic

1 teaspoon salt

2 tablespoons chopped fresh cilantro

Black pepper

1 Bring large saucepan of salted water to a boil over medium-high heat. Add beans; cook 6 minutes or until tender. Drain beans.

2 Meanwhile, melt butter in large skillet over medium-high heat. Add bell pepper and onion; cook and stir 3 minutes or until vegetables are tender but not browned. Add garlic; cook and stir 30 seconds. Add beans and salt; cook and stir 2 minutes or until beans are heated through and coated with butter.

3 Stir in cilantro; season with black pepper. Serve immediately.

Green Chile Rice
makes 4 to 6 servings

1 can (about 14 ounces) chicken broth plus water to measure 2 cups

1 cup uncooked rice

1 can (4 ounces) diced mild green chiles

½ medium yellow onion, diced

1 teaspoon dried oregano

½ teaspoon salt

½ teaspoon cumin seeds

3 green onions, thinly sliced

⅓ to ½ cup chopped fresh cilantro

1 Combine broth, rice, chiles, yellow onion, oregano, salt and cumin seeds in large saucepan; bring to a boil over high heat.

2 Reduce heat to low; cover and simmer 18 minutes or until liquid is absorbed and rice is tender.

3 Fluff rice with fork; stir in green onions and cilantro.

Buckwheat with Zucchini and Mushrooms
makes 4 to 6 servings

1½ tablespoons olive oil

1 cup sliced mushrooms

1 medium zucchini, cut into ½-inch pieces

1 medium onion, chopped

1 clove garlic, minced

¾ cup buckwheat

¾ teaspoon salt

¼ teaspoon dried thyme

⅛ teaspoon black pepper

1¼ cups vegetable broth

Lemon wedges (optional)

1 Heat oil in large skillet over medium heat. Add mushrooms, zucchini, onion and garlic; cook 7 to 10 minutes or until vegetables are tender, stirring occasionally.

2 Add buckwheat, salt, thyme and pepper; cook and stir 2 minutes.

3 Stir in broth; bring to a boil. Reduce heat to low; cover and cook 10 to 13 minutes or until liquid is absorbed and buckwheat is tender. Remove from heat; let stand, covered, 5 minutes. Serve with lemon wedges, if desired.

Tip

For extra flavor, add pancetta to this dish. Before cooking the vegetables, coarsely chop 4 slices pancetta; cook and stir about 5 minutes. Add 1 tablespoon olive oil, mushrooms, zucchini, onion and garlic to the skillet; proceed as directed above.

Roasted Red Potatoes >
makes 4 servings

2 pounds unpeeled small red potatoes, cut into halves (or quarters if potatoes are larger than 1 inch)

2 tablespoons olive oil

1 teaspoon salt

¾ teaspoon smoked paprika

¼ teaspoon black pepper

1 Preheat oven to 425°F. Spray baking sheet with nonstick cooking spray.

2 Combine potatoes, oil, salt, paprika and pepper in medium bowl; toss to coat. Spread potatoes cut sides down in single layer on prepared baking sheet.

3 Roast 25 minutes or until bottoms are browned. Turn and roast 10 minutes or until potatoes are tender.

Bulgur Pilaf with Caramelized Onions and Kale
makes 4 to 6 servings

1 tablespoon olive oil

1 small onion, cut into thin wedges

1 clove garlic, minced

2 cups chopped kale

2 cups vegetable broth

¾ cup medium grain bulgur

½ teaspoon salt

¼ teaspoon black pepper

1 Heat oil in large skillet over medium heat. Add onion; cook 8 minutes or until softened and lightly browned, stirring frequently. Add garlic; cook and stir 1 minute. Add kale; cook and stir about 1 minute or until kale is wilted.

2 Stir in broth, bulgur, salt and pepper; bring to a boil. Reduce heat to low; cover and simmer 12 minutes or until liquid is absorbed and bulgur is tender.

Refried Beans >
makes 4 to 6 servings

2 tablespoons vegetable oil

1 can (28 ounces) pinto beans, rinsed and drained*

½ cup water

Salt and black pepper

Crumbled cotija cheese or queso fresco (optional)

Or substitute two cans (about 15 ounces each) pinto beans.

1 Heat oil in large skillet over medium-high heat. Add beans and water; mash and stir with potato masher until beans reach desired consistency. Cook about 5 minutes or until heated through, adding additional water if beans seem dry.

2 Taste and season with salt and pepper. Sprinkle with cheese, if desired.

Roasted Balsamic Asparagus
makes 4 to 6 servings

1 pound fresh asparagus

1 tablespoon olive oil

½ teaspoon salt

¼ teaspoon black pepper

1 tablespoon balsamic glaze*

¼ cup shredded or grated Parmesan cheese

Balsamic glaze can be found in the condiment section of the supermarket or can be prepared by simmering 2 tablespoons balsamic vinegar until reduced by about half.

1 Preheat oven to 375°F.

2 Place asparagus in single layer in shallow 11×7-inch baking dish or on baking sheet. Drizzle with oil; toss gently to coat. Sprinkle with salt and pepper.

3 Roast 14 to 16 minutes or until asparagus is crisp-tender. Drizzle with balsamic glaze; roll with tongs to coat. Sprinkle with cheese.

Garlic Fries
makes 4 servings

2 large potatoes,
   peeled and cut into
   matchstick strips

2 teaspoons plus
   1 tablespoon olive oil,
   divided

1½ teaspoons minced garlic

½ teaspoon dried parsley

½ teaspoon salt

¼ teaspoon ground
   black pepper

   Ketchup and/or blue
   cheese dressing
   (optional)

1 Preheat oven to 400°F. Line baking sheet with parchment paper.

2 Combine potatoes and 2 teaspoons oil in medium bowl; toss to coat. Spread potatoes in single layer on prepared baking sheet.

3 Bake 15 to 20 minutes or until potatoes are golden brown and crisp.

4 Meanwhile, combine remaining 1 tablespoon oil, garlic, parsley, salt and pepper in small bowl; mix well. Add warm potatoes to garlic mixture; toss to coat. Serve immediately with desired sauces.

Green Beans and Mushrooms >
makes 4 to 6 servings

1½ tablespoons olive oil, divided

1 small onion, thinly sliced

8 ounces sliced mushrooms

¾ teaspoon salt, divided

1 pound fresh green beans, trimmed

1 teaspoon minced garlic

¼ teaspoon black pepper

1 Heat 1 tablespoon oil in large skillet over medium-high heat. Add onion; cook and stir 2 minutes or until beginning to soften. Add mushrooms and ¼ teaspoon salt; cook about 5 minutes or until mushrooms give off liquid and begin to brown, stirring occasionally.

2 Add green beans and remaining ½ tablespoon oil to skillet; cook and stir 3 minutes. Reduce heat to medium-low; cover and cook 10 to 12 minutes or until beans are crisp-tender.

3 Stir in garlic, remaining ½ teaspoon salt and pepper; cook and stir 2 minutes.

Glazed Maple Acorn Squash
makes 4 servings

1 large acorn squash

¼ cup water

2 tablespoons pure maple syrup

1 tablespoon butter, melted

¼ teaspoon ground cinnamon

⅛ teaspoon salt

1 Preheat oven to 375°F.

2 Cut stem and blossom ends from squash. Cut squash crosswise into four slices; discard seeds and membrane. Pour water into 13×9-inch baking dish. Place squash in baking dish; cover with foil.

3 Bake 30 minutes or until tender.

4 Combine maple syrup, butter, cinnamon and salt in small bowl; mix well. Uncover squash; pour off water. Brush squash with syrup mixture, letting excess pool in center of squash rings. Bake 10 minutes or until syrup mixture is bubbly.

Index

Index

Index

Index

Metric Conversion Chart

VOLUME MEASUREMENTS (dry)

$\frac{1}{8}$ teaspoon = 0.5 mL
$\frac{1}{4}$ teaspoon = 1 mL
$\frac{1}{2}$ teaspoon = 2 mL
$\frac{3}{4}$ teaspoon = 4 mL
1 teaspoon = 5 mL
1 tablespoon = 15 mL
2 tablespoons = 30 mL
$\frac{1}{4}$ cup = 60 mL
$\frac{1}{3}$ cup = 75 mL
$\frac{1}{2}$ cup = 125 mL
$\frac{2}{3}$ cup = 150 mL
$\frac{3}{4}$ cup = 175 mL
1 cup = 250 mL
2 cups = 1 pint = 500 mL
3 cups = 750 mL
4 cups = 1 quart = 1 L

VOLUME MEASUREMENTS (fluid)

1 fluid ounce (2 tablespoons) = 30 mL
4 fluid ounces ($\frac{1}{2}$ cup) = 125 mL
8 fluid ounces (1 cup) = 250 mL
12 fluid ounces ($1\frac{1}{2}$ cups) = 375 mL
16 fluid ounces (2 cups) = 500 mL

WEIGHTS (mass)

$\frac{1}{2}$ ounce = 15 g
1 ounce = 30 g
3 ounces = 90 g
4 ounces = 120 g
8 ounces = 225 g
10 ounces = 285 g
12 ounces = 360 g
16 ounces = 1 pound = 450 g

DIMENSIONS

$\frac{1}{16}$ inch = 2 mm
$\frac{1}{8}$ inch = 3 mm
$\frac{1}{4}$ inch = 6 mm
$\frac{1}{2}$ inch = 1.5 cm
$\frac{3}{4}$ inch = 2 cm
1 inch = 2.5 cm

OVEN TEMPERATURES

250°F = 120°C
275°F = 140°C
300°F = 150°C
325°F = 160°C
350°F = 180°C
375°F = 190°C
400°F = 200°C
425°F = 220°C
450°F = 230°C

BAKING PAN SIZES

Utensil	Size in Inches/Quarts	Metric Volume	Size in Centimeters
Baking or Cake Pan (square or rectangular)	8×8×2	2 L	20×20×5
	9×9×2	2.5 L	23×23×5
	12×8×2	3 L	30×20×5
	13×9×2	3.5 L	33×23×5
Loaf Pan	8×4×3	1.5 L	20×10×7
	9×5×3	2 L	23×13×7
Round Layer Cake Pan	8×1½	1.2 L	20×4
	9×1½	1.5 L	23×4
Pie Plate	8×1¼	750 mL	20×3
	9×1¼	1 L	23×3
Baking Dish or Casserole	1 quart	1 L	—
	1½ quart	1.5 L	—
	2 quart	2 L	—